Informal Workers and a Political Economy of Lifelong Learning

Seth Brown · Peter Kelly · Scott K. Phillips

Informal Workers and a Political Economy of Lifelong Learning

Provocations from the Margins of Global Capitalism

Seth Brown
School of Education
RMIT University
Bundoora, VIC, Australia

Peter Kelly
School of Education
Deakin University
Waurn Ponds, VIC, Australia

Scott K. Phillips
Kershaw Phillips Consulting
Williamstown, VIC, Australia

RMIT University
Bundoora, VIC, Australia

ISBN 978-3-031-72450-3   ISBN 978-3-031-72451-0   (eBook)
https://doi.org/10.1007/978-3-031-72451-0

© The Editor(s) (if applicable) and The Author(s), under exclusive license to Springer Nature Switzerland AG 2024

This work is subject to copyright. All rights are solely and exclusively licensed by the Publisher, whether the whole or part of the material is concerned, specifically the rights of translation, reprinting, reuse of illustrations, recitation, broadcasting, reproduction on microfilms or in any other physical way, and transmission or information storage and retrieval, electronic adaptation, computer software, or by similar or dissimilar methodology now known or hereafter developed.
The use of general descriptive names, registered names, trademarks, service marks, etc. in this publication does not imply, even in the absence of a specific statement, that such names are exempt from the relevant protective laws and regulations and therefore free for general use.
The publisher, the authors and the editors are safe to assume that the advice and information in this book are believed to be true and accurate at the date of publication. Neither the publisher nor the authors or the editors give a warranty, expressed or implied, with respect to the material contained herein or for any errors or omissions that may have been made. The publisher remains neutral with regard to jurisdictional claims in published maps and institutional affiliations.

Cover illustration: © Harvey Loake

This Palgrave Macmillan imprint is published by the registered company Springer Nature Switzerland AG
The registered company address is: Gewerbestrasse 11, 6330 Cham, Switzerland

If disposing of this product, please recycle the paper.

Seth: For Soraya and Star
Peter: For Georgia and Julie
Scott: For Susan, Natalie and Des, Tim and Alice, Claudia, Leo, and Lila

Acknowledgements

Seth and Scott acknowledge the School of Education and UNEVOC Centre at RMIT for their support of our involvement in this project.

Peter also acknowledges the School of Education and the Centre for Research for Educational Impact at Deakin University for their support of his involvement in this project.

Contents

1 **Informal Economies and Informal Workers in Global Capitalism** — 1
  Introduction: Wasted Lives? — 2
  The Informal Economy, Informal Workers and Lifelong Learning — 5
  A Political Economy of Lifelong Learning (LLL) — 9
  Structure of the Book — 12
  References — 17

2 **Latin America and the Caribbean (LAC)** — 21
  Introduction — 25
  The Informal Sector and Skills Training in LAC — 26
  Pandemic Recovery and a New Skills and VET Agenda for LAC? — 31
     Investment in Education and Training — 33
     Lifelong Learning — 33
     Technological Replacement of Routine Tasks/Jobs — 34
     Active Labour Market Programmes — 34
     Social Protection — 34
  Provocation: "Disaster Capitalism" and Elements of a Political Economy of Lifelong Learning in LAC — 35
  References — 40

3 The Middle East and North Africa (MENA) — 43
Introduction — 47
The Informal Sector and Skills Training in MENA — 48
Pathways to Social and Economic Justice for Informal Workers: Partnerships for Creating Local Learning and Skills Development — 55
Provocation: A Political Economy of Lifelong Learning (LLL) in the Context of Conflict and Digital Revolutions — 59
References — 63

4 Sub-Saharan Africa (SSA) — 65
Introduction — 69
The Informal Sector and Skills Training in SSA — 71
Creating a More Prosperous, Inclusive and Sustainable SSA? — 74
Provocation: A New VET Agenda for SSA: Beyond Productivism and Extractivism? — 77
    Gulu — 81
    Hoima — 82
    Durban — 82
    Alice — 83
References — 85

5 Central and Eastern Europe (CEE) — 89
Introduction — 96
The Informal Sector and Skills Training in CEE — 97
Creating Enabling Environments for Informal Workers' Lifelong Learning — 102
Provocation: A Political Economy of Lifelong Learning in the CEE Region — 106
References — 110

6 The Asia–Pacific Region — 113
Introduction — 116
The Informal Sector and Skills Training in the Asia–Pacific Region — 118
Economic Growth, the Informal Sector and the Limits of the Digitalisation of Lifelong Learning in the Asia–Pacific Region — 121
Provocation: The "Broken Promise" of Lifelong Learning? — 126
References — 131

7 **A Political Economy of Lifelong Learning (LLL) for Decent Work and Just Transitions?**   137
Introduction   138
Skills and Training for Decent Work and Just Transitions   143
  Policy, Systems and Institutions   144
  Vocational Knowledge   145
  Critical Capabilities Approach (CCA) and VET for Community Development   147
  Skills for Sustainable Development   151
References   154

Index   159

CHAPTER 1

Informal Economies and Informal Workers in Global Capitalism

Abstract This chapter introduces the aims and purposes of this book, and presents an overview of key dimensions of the challenges and opportunities that were amplified by the social, cultural, economic and political consequences of the COVID-19 pandemic as these continue to shape and echo through the informal economies, and the experiences of informal workers, of Latin America and the Caribbean (LAC), the Middle East and North Africa (MENA), Sub-Saharan Africa (SSA), Central and Eastern Europe (CEE) and the Asia–Pacific (AP). The chapter frames this discussion through an engagement with the ways in which skills, education and training and contested ideas about Lifelong Learning (LLL) are understood as being central to the problem of "informality", and as the "panacea" to this problem. It also introduces our argument that conceiving of these challenges and opportunities as being structured by a "political economy" of LLL provides a productive avenue by which we can draw on diverse, but critical, theoretical and methodological tools in developing our analysis in the chapters that follow.

Keywords Informal economy · Informal workers · Skills development · Political economy · Lifelong Learning · "Wasted lives"

Introduction: *Wasted Lives?*

In *Working in Jamie's Kitchen: Salvation Passion and Young Workers* we (Kelly & Harrison, 2009) developed a critical analysis of the ways in which the UK celebrity chef Jamie Oliver, and his hospitality and training social enterprise The Fifteen Foundation developed a hospitality-based training programme for, in the first instance, unemployed young Londoners and, later, other groups of young people at training restaurants in the UK, the US and Australia.

That book was fundamentally concerned with identifying and exploring such things as: ideas about the passion that unemployed young people should develop for food and work as it was imagined by Jamie Oliver; the forms of entrepreneurial selfhood that unemployed young people should develop; the entanglements of gender, class and ethnicity with these ideas of passion and enterprise; the generational understandings of unemployed young people's apparent lack of passion and enterprise in relation to food and work; and the roles that training and skills development could play in fostering passion and enterprise in young people for these things so that they might secure some form of parlous, earthbound salvation through participation in the world of paid work.

In pursuing these concerns we were drawn to the sociology of Zygmunt Bauman—the influential sociologist of liquid modernity. In *Wasted Lives: Modernity and its Outcasts* (2004) Bauman had argued that at the start of the twenty-first century large numbers of people around the globe—hundreds of millions, in fact—are surplus to requirements, are, indeed, redundant. Bauman (2004, pp. 5–6) argued that this redundancy is a consequence of the global spread and triumph of modernisation processes: "The production of 'human waste'...(the 'excessive' and 'redundant', that is the population of those who either could not or were not wished to be recognised or allowed to stay), is an inevitable outcome of modernization". For Bauman, these modernisation processes can, largely, be understood in terms of the colonisation of all aspects of life, of all spaces and places by market forces, practices and processes under regimes of capital accumulation. As processes of modernisation have become truly globalised, as the "totality of human production and consumption has become money and market mediated, and the processes of the commodification, commercialization and monetarization of human livelihoods have penetrated every nook and cranny of the globe", then the "crisis of the human waste disposal industry" has become more acute.

A key element to Bauman's (2004, pp. 5–7) argument is that the history of European colonisation is a history characterised by exporting "redundant humans" to the pre-modern, so-called under-developed spaces of the Americas, Africa, Asia and the Pacific. The triumphant globalisation of modernisation has resulted not only in the continued (over) production of wasted lives in the high-income economies of the OECD and the EU (the West), but also the disappearance of a colonial solution to waste disposal. Moreover, the figures of the immigrant, the asylum seeker and the refugee represent the reversal of the flows of waste disposal: a reversal that provokes fear and anxiety in the imaginations of the twenty-first-century inhabitants of the affluent, but increasingly insecure, West.

Being surplus to requirements, being redundant, means that individuals, even entire populations, are confronted with the possibility that their way of life does not provide the means to secure a livelihood. The idea of redundancy, the reality that you, or I, or we might be in-excess, is a powerful and disturbing concept and reality. In the first instance the concept of redundancy says something, means something, different to the concept of unemployment. Importantly, for Bauman (2004, pp. 11–12), this concept says something different in a particular time and space (the affluent West at the turn of a millennium); and speaks powerfully to a particular generation: "How different is the idea of 'redundancy' that has shot into prominence during the lifetime of Generation X! Where the prefix 'un' in 'unemployment' used to suggest a departure from the norm—as in 'unhealthy' or 'unwell'—there is no such suggestion in the notion of 'redundancy'". Rather, as Bauman indicates, redundancy "whispers permanence and hints at the ordinariness of the condition". In this sense redundant "names a condition without offering a ready-to-use antonym".

Redundancy, the sense that you, or I, or we are of limited or no use—particularly in social, cultural and commercial environments in which usefulness not only brings material rewards, but also gives purpose and meaning to a life—can have profound consequences for a sense of self. As Bauman (2004, p. 12) suggests: "To be 'redundant' means to be supernumerary, unneeded, of no use—whatever the needs and uses are that set the standard of usefulness and indispensability. The others do not need you; they can do as well, and better, without you". What is more, to be redundant suggests that there is no "self-evident reason for your being around and no obvious justification for your claim to have the right to stay around". In this sense, to be "declared redundant means to have been disposed of because of being disposable—just like the empty and non-refundable plastic bottle or once-used syringe, an unattractive commodity with no buyers". For Bauman (2004, p. 12) redundancy, as a concept (but also, significantly, as a state of being) shares its "semantic space with 'rejects', 'wastrels', 'garbage', 'refuse'—with waste". To be redundant or surplus to requirements holds out different possibilities or prospects to being unemployed: "The destination of the unemployed, of the 'reserve army of labour', was to be called back into active service. The destination of waste is the waste yard, the rubbish heap".

In building on these initial provocations—which are *not* about a sense that an individual's life might be a "waste", but that at the start of the twenty-first century, globalising "modernisation" processes condemn billions of people to live lives on the margins of these processes in largely unregulated economies and forms of labour that offer few protections, and/or the rights and privileges afforded workers in more regulated economies and labour markets—we want to introduce some of the key conceptual concerns of this book.

Our primary purpose here is to present an overview of key dimensions of the challenges and opportunities that were, that continue to be, amplified by the social, cultural, economic and political consequences of the COVID-19 pandemic as these continue to echo through and shape the informal economies, and the experiences of informal workers, of Latin America and the Caribbean (LAC), the Middle East and North Africa (MENA), Sub-Saharan Africa (SSA), Central and Eastern Europe (CEE) and the Asia–Pacific (AP). We frame this discussion through an engagement with the ways in which skills, education and training and contested ideas about Lifelong Learning (LLL) are understood as being central to the problem of "informality", and as the "panacea" to this problem.

Our focus on these regions is not unproblematic. These regional groupings—which can tend to gloss over significant differences among member countries of these regions, and suggest a homogeneity where there is diversity and difference—are, often, "administrative" artefacts of the United Nations and its agencies. These administrative and organisational logics then compel other organisations and agencies—such as, for example, the World Bank, the International Monetary Fund, the OECD and the EU—to use these groupings both for internal and comparative purposes. As we progress through the chapters that follow, we highlight some of the challenges and opportunities that are associated with using these groupings.

The book also seeks to highlight historical and contemporary characteristics of informality in different regions, including the ways in which the COVID-19 pandemic, and the public health, social and economic policy responses to the pandemic, have impacted informal workers in different regions in different ways. A report from the ILO (2021b, p. 19), for example, points to the fact that 70% of the global working-age population (4 billion people) have little or no safety net, leaving only 30% "legally covered by comprehensive social security systems...with women's coverage lagging behind men's" (ILO, 2021b, p. 19). There are significant challenges across and within regions "with coverage rates in Europe and Central Asia (83.9 per cent) and the Americas (64.3 per cent) above the global average, while Asia and the Pacific (44.1 per cent), the Arab States (40.0 per cent) and Africa (17.4 per cent) have far more marked coverage gaps".

In doing this work, our analysis will draw on, variously and at different times, theories of post- and neo-colonialism, space, place and globalisation, critical accounts of curriculum and pedagogy in skills and vocational education and training, the critical literature on sustainable development, the Sustainable Development Goals (SDGs) and Lifelong Learning (LLL) and theories and observations about the future of work and the convergence of the Fourth Industrial Revolution and the 6th Mass Extinction, a convergence "between an advanced knowledge economy, which perpetuates patterns of discrimination and exclusion, and the threat of climate change devastation for both human and non-human entities" (Braidotti, 2019, n.p.).

The Informal Economy, Informal Workers and Lifelong Learning

The informal economy, the informal workers that comprise the labour force for the informal economy, the relationships between these informal sectors and workers and more formal sectors and workers, are complex and difficult to develop shared agreement and understandings in relation to. Indeed, in many of the high-income, formalised and regulated economies of the OECD and EU, new forms of precarious, informal and uncertain employment—the so-called gig economy—have emerged in the context of, and been energised by, processes of neoliberal globalisation and governmentalities. In *The Brazilianisation of Youth Transitions in Australia and the UK?*, for example, we (Furlong & Kelly, 2005) explored the ways in which these forms of precarious, 'gig' work were transforming youth labour markets in Australia and the UK. The title for that paper came from Ulrich Beck's (2000) *The Brave New World of Work*. A central theme of Beck's book is that labour markets in the more developed "first world" had been changing during the last four decades in ways that witnessed them taking on some of the central characteristics of labour markets in what was then called the less-developed "third world"—what Beck refers to as the *Brazilianisation* of labour markets in the developed world. For Beck (2000, p. 1), what was central to these transformations was the "spread of temporary and insecure employment, discontinuity and loose informality" into "first world" labour markets—which for the period of three decades or so after the Second World War had been the "bastions of full employment". Beck's (2000, p. 1) argument was that in a "semi-industrialized" economy such as Brazil, full-time waged or salaried employment is a secure form of existence for "only a minority of the economically active population; the majority earn their living in more precarious conditions". For Beck (2000, pp. 2–3) a life world characterised by "nomadic 'multi-activity'" is not a "pre-modern relic", nor is it any longer just a feature of the female labour market. Rather, this precariousness and insecurity emerges in the more developed world as a fundamental characteristic of the movement from a *work society* to a *risk society*.

In the economies of the OECD and the EU, and in the more informal economies of Latin America and the Caribbean (LAC), the Middle East and North Africa (MENA), Sub-Saharan Africa (SSA), Central and Eastern Europe (CEE) and the Asia–Pacific (AP) that are our focus here, the challenges and opportunities of/for promoting *sustained, inclusive and sustainable economic growth, full and productive employment and decent work for all* (UN SDG8) are connected to broader concerns in relation to social, economic and political development—as captured at a global level in the 2030 Agenda for Sustainable Development. Although it may be understood in different ways in these different contexts, and, indeed, will be situated differently in particular contexts, we understand the informal economy as those:

economic activities by workers that are—in law or in practice—not covered (or insufficiently covered) by formal employment arrangements. Although it is hard to generalize about the quality and nature of informal employment, the characteristics include a lack of protection for non-payment of wages, retrenchment without notice or compensation, unsatisfactory occupational health and safety conditions and an absence of social benefits such as pensions, sick pay and health insurance. (ILO, 2021a)

The ILO's (2018a) *Women and men in the informal economy: A statistical picture* provides a description of various key characteristics of the informal economy and informal workers on a global and regional scale that are important for what follows:

- *The Size of the Informal Economy*
  Two billion of the world's employed population aged 15 and over work informally, representing 61.2% of global employment. Among the five main regions, the vast majority of employment in Africa (85.8%) is informal. Asia and the Pacific (68.2%) and the Arab States (68.6 %) have almost the same level of informality. In the Americas and Europe and Central Asia, less than half of employment is informal.
- *Socio-Economic Development and Informality*
  Emerging and developing countries represent 82% of world employment...More than two-thirds of the employed population in emerging and developing countries are in informal employment (69.6%).
- *Economic Sector and Informality*
  Informal employment can be in the informal sector, in the formal sector or in the household sector. The 61.2% of global employment that is informal is comprised of 51.9% in the informal sector, 6.7% in the formal sector and 2.5% in households.
- *Employment Status and Informality*
  The employment status category with the highest percentage of informality is own-account workers, both globally and regionally. Globally, 86.1% of own-account workers are informal.
- *Age of Workers and Informality*
  The level of informality is higher among young people and older persons. Worldwide three out of four young (77.1%) and older persons (77.9%) are in informal employment.

- *Education and Informality*
    Globally, when the level of education increases, the level of informality decreases. Those who have completed secondary and tertiary education are less likely to be in informal employment compared to workers who have either no education or completed primary education.
- *Gender and Informality*
    Globally, the share of women in informal employment is lower than the share of men…but…women are indeed more exposed to informal employment in more than 90% of Sub-Saharan African countries, 89% of countries from Southern Asia and almost 75% of Latin American countries.

As Alla-Mensah and McGrath (2023) observe, various agencies, including the ILO, acknowledge that these gross figures do not tell the whole story of informality. Some research cautions against making "judgements" based on these sorts of statistical overviews. Kanbur (2021, p. 3), for example, suggests that any discourse on informality should avoid:

> the common notion that there is something inherently "bad" or "problematic" about informality. As we shall see, this is a historical legacy from colonial times that still governs the administrative mindset. "Reducing informality" per se is not an appropriate objective. Rather, the framework calls for the design of regulation and interventions with appropriate social objectives, taking into account economic and social agents' varied responses.

Many observers, agencies, researchers and commentators offer various proposals for meeting these challenges. Given the diversity of these proposals, and the diversity of contexts in which these interventions are conceived, developed and deployed, it is productive to group many of them under the banner of the concept of Lifelong Learning (LLL). This focus on a concept such as LLL enables us to connect to a key focus of a range of individuals, organisations, agencies and governments in addressing the challenges and opportunities of the informal economy from a sustainable development perspective. The ILO (2019, pp. 30–32) suggests that:

Lifelong learning encompasses formal and informal learning from early childhood and basic education through to adult learning, combining foundation skills, social and cognitive skills (such as learning to learn) and the skills needed for specific jobs, occupations or sectors.
Lifelong learning involves more than the skills needed to work; it is also about developing the capabilities needed to participate in a democratic society.
It offers a pathway to inclusion in labour markets for youth and the unemployed.
It also has transformative potential: investment in learning at an early age facilitates learning at later stages in life and is in turn linked to intergenerational social mobility, expanding the choices of future generations.

From this perspective, LLL can be understood, by extension, as learning that is "not only lifelong, starting in childhood and extending to adulthood, but also 'life-wide', 'occurring not only formally in schools and higher education, but also non formally and informally in the home, community and workplaces'" (Palmer, 2020, p. 7). The SDGs commit—particularly through a number of targets identified under SDG 4, 5 and 8—to a "universal entitlement" to LLL and decent work for all in economic, social, cultural and political processes that promise the possibility of sustainable development.

However, the core logic of these commitments arises from the fact that billions of people around the globe do not enjoy the relevant entitlements, or the benefits that promise to flow from their enjoyment. And this inequity continues, despite the UN member country governments, intergovernmental agencies, philanthropic and aid agencies, businesses, communities and individuals making commitments to the 2030 Agenda for Sustainable Development. It is these "realities" that provide both a point of departure, and a warrant, for the exploration of the political economy of LLL that we undertake here.

A POLITICAL ECONOMY OF LIFELONG LEARNING (LLL)

Given this outline of the things that interest us here, and going back once again to Bauman's (2004) observations and critique of the globalising processes that condemn, or threaten to condemn, many billions of people to live lives on the margins of these processes in largely unregulated economies and forms of labour that offer few protections, and/or the rights and privileges afforded workers in more regulated economies and labour markets, we want to suggest that conceiving of these challenges and opportunities as being structured by a "political economy" of Lifelong Learning (LLL) provides a productive avenue by which we can draw on diverse, but critical, theoretical and methodological tools in developing our analysis in what follows.

The sense that a particular orientation to "political economy" opens up our work to theoretical and methodological "pluralism" emerges from earlier contributions that we have made to debates about a "political economy of youth" (Kelly, 2018, pp. 1285–1287). In that contribution we outlined "three notes on a political economy of youth", which we identified as:

1. Capitalism: From the First Industrial Revolution to the Third Industrial Revolution;
2. Youth as an artefact of governmentalised expertise;
3. The agency/structure problem in youth studies: Foucault's dispositif and post-human exceptionalism.

The details of these notes are not of direct interest at this time, although aspects of them will feature at different times in what follows. At that time, we suggested that Maysoun Sukarieh and Stuart Tannock (2015, 2016), in the context of what had developed as an oftentimes acrimonious and somewhat limited "debate", provided a productive definition of what a political economy of youth might look like that suggested possibilities for moving the discussion forward. In developing their approach to political economy, they referenced the Political Economy Project (2017) of the Arab Studies Institute (Washington and Beirut), and a definition of political economy that explicitly draws on the "intellectual tradition of political economy from Karl Marx to the present, embracing both its methodological pluralism and its fundamental critique of capital and empire". In this sense political economy:

> addresses the mutual constitution of states, markets, and classes, the co-constitution of class, race, gender, and other forms of identity, varying modes of capital accumulation and the legal, political, and cultural forms of their regulation, relations among local, national, and global forms of capital, class, and culture, the construction of forms of knowledge and hegemony; techno-politics; water and the environment as resources and fields of contestation; the role of war in the constitution of states and

classes; and practices and cultures of domination and resistance. (Arab Studies Institute, 2017, n.p.)

As we observed at that time, no single theoretical, methodological and/or empirical approach is equipped to do all this work, at all times, in all places. Instead, the argument could be made that diverse approaches—each and all with a variety of interests in identifying, examining and analysing the array of conditions in which young people, their families and peers live their lives and conduct relationships in complex and differing communities, neighbourhoods, educational institutions, workplaces, digital and non-digital spaces; the forms of social, cultural, economic and political regulation, government, surveillance and policy that shape, even control these circumstances; and the diverse, often horrendously disadvantaged and marginalised, consequences (intended or otherwise) of these practices, processes and relations—have something to contribute to a political economy of youth. As we observed, this is not to say that all youth studies have such interests. Again, Sukarieh and Tannock (2016, p. 1282), drawing on Mosco's (2009, pp. 3–4, 26) *Political Economy of Communication*, suggest a way forward here, indicating that:

> political economy approaches tend to be distinguished by the relative degree of attention paid to the relationship between local settings and 'the totality of social relations that make up the economic, political, social, and cultural areas of life', as well as long-term patterns of 'social change and historical transformation'.

Part of the logic of framing our contribution through these "three notes" was to bring together diverse, but related, aspects of the work that we have done over a number of years to suggest that at the start of the twenty-first century, capitalism is globalising, is largely neoliberal—that is, a form of capitalism that is individualised and privatised, where all that can be is commodified and subjected to a competitive, market logic, where individuals and communities are made responsible for aspects of a life that completely elude limited capacities for what some call "agency" (Beck, 1992, 2000; Bauman 2001; Kelly 2013, 2017)—and is being reconfigured in profound ways by Anthropogenic climate change, bio-genetics and Artificial Intelligence (AI). As we argued there, and in ways that can mirror our approach to developing a political economy of LLL, a political economy of twenty-first-century capitalism, must be able to account for a capitalism that in many ways looks like the capitalism of the first and second Industrial Revolutions (the capitalism of Marx and Weber), but which is at the same time profoundly different as it enters what is variously described as the Third/Fourth Industrial Revolution or the 2nd Machine Age (Lanchester, 2015; Rifkin, 2011; WEF, 2020). There, and here, we can suggest that it is these profound emergences that pose the greatest challenges for engaging with a political economy of youth and of LLL. It is in this sense that we imagine the plurality of critical, theoretical and methodological challenges and possibilities that we will use to structure the analysis that we develop in what follows.

These ideas have emerged from and been developed through an encounter with a number of productive trajectories suggested by authors such as Simon McGrath, Presha Ramsarup, Jacques Zeelenc, Volker Wedekind, Stephanie Allais, Heila Lotz-Sisitka, David Monk, George Openjuru and Jo-Anna Russon, and their work on a political economy of LLL and VET for sustainable development, decent work and just transitions in Africa. Foundational to this political economy of LLL is identifying what the concept of "skills for just transitions" might mean, might look like, in "complex labour market and vocational learning contexts" (McGrath & Russon, 2023, p. 4). For Mark Swilling (2020, p. 7), the concept of "just transitions" signals "a process of increasingly radical incremental changes that accumulate over time in the actually emergent transformed world envisaged by the SDGs and sustainability". This concept of a political economy of LLL for decent work and just transitions will be an important thread in what follows—and it will be more fully explored in Chapters 4 and 7.

Structure of the Book

Each chapter in the book will begin with a "story" that seeks to highlight a more particular concern—often geographically located, but sometimes about an issue or theme—that enables us to open a space to develop a critical engagement with various academic, policy and international agency discourses that frame particular responses to the challenges and opportunities that shape the education and training opportunities, informal economies and the experiences of informal workers, of Latin America and the Caribbean (LAC), the Middle East and North Africa (MENA),

Sub-Saharan Africa (SSA), Central and Eastern Europe (CEE) and the Asia–Pacific (AP). Each chapter will also include a provocation that seeks to build on this story, and frame the contribution that we seek to make to exploring particular dimensions of a political economy of LLL in that region. Importantly, this framing of the arguments of the book will foreshadow, through the various provocations introduced in each chapter, the discussion in the concluding chapter in which we will turn to a model for rethinking Lifelong Learning (LLL) and skills and training for informal economy workers that promises transformative progress towards the Agenda for Sustainable Development.

In *Chapter 2: Latin America and the Caribbean (LAC)* we reference the substantial academic and grey literature that suggests that the informal sector in Latin America and the Caribbean (LAC) was "estimated to represent around half of total employment", and that the COVID-19 crisis has amplified the scale, scope and character of the informal economy, indicating that informal employment is the most pervasive "structural weakness" in the LAC economies (Basto-Aguirre et al., 2020; OECD, 2020a, 2020b). As Basto-Aguirre et al. (2020, n. p.) suggest:

> Both cause and consequence of many of the regions' development traps...informality has been eroding tax collection, undermining productivity growth, and leaving a large share of the workforce vulnerable to shocks for lack of social protection, while feeding on low productivity levels, unsophisticated economic structures, rigid regulations, low skill levels and inefficient institutions.

Our provocation in this chapter suggests that the challenges faced by informal workers in the informal economies of LAC appear not to be amenable to the sorts of remedies that organisations such as the World Bank propose. Indeed, the historical actions of many of these organisations and agencies have produced the forces and processes that continue to energise these seemingly intractable, "wicked problems". We explore a number of these concerns via reference to Naomi Klein's (2007) *The Shock Doctrine: The Rise of Disaster Capitalism*, and how her detailed, extensive and highly critical account of the influence of the Chicago School of Economics and the Washington Consensus in shaping the LAC's "lost decade" can inform a political economy of LLL in LAC.

Chapter 3: The Middle East and North Africa (MENA) takes up the issues we are interested in within the region that comprises the Gulf States and the Arab states of North Africa. Informal employment in MENA is widespread, and accounts for 68% of total employment—up to 78% in Yemen and 81% in Morocco (OECD, 2020a, p. 1). In 2019, 30% of young people aged 15–24 were unemployed or not in school or receiving any training and for women who have the lowest employment rates in the world the number rises to 42% with young people in general three times more likely to be unemployed than older workers (ILO et al., 2023).

In the third chapter we note there are often conflicting accounts about the challenges facing informal workers in the MENA region. While Ohnsorge and Yu (2022, pp. 225–226) argue that the main drivers of informality include limited private sector activity, armed conflict, human capital deficits, low labour productivity and wages and less inclusive growth. A more critical, political economy perspective suggests "perhaps the widening share of informal labour in Arab countries in non-agricultural sectors is mainly the result of policies of 'Openness', neo-liberal globalization, youth boom, rural migration in great numbers as a result of neglecting rural areas in general and the agriculture sector in particular, in addition to large waves of incoming migration" (Safa, 2018, p. 1). Building on these accounts, our provocation in this chapter argues that the skills needs of informal workers (especially young people) have to be understood in the context of the political economy of MENA, and the ways that lifelong learning approaches can assist them to adapt to the changing structure and opportunities associated with the Fourth Industrial Revolution as well as the aftermath of conflicts such as between Israel and Hamas in Gaza.

As we will demonstrate in *Chapter 4: Sub-Saharan Africa (SSA)*, the informal economy, particularly in urban contexts, is "the main source of employment and the backbone of economic activity" (Guven & Karlen, 2020; Kiaga, 2020). Indeed, "Eight out of ten workers in Africa are in informal employment, the highest share among all regions" (Kiaga & Leung, 2020, p. 3). In SSA, as Kiaga and Leung (2020, p. 11) observe, there are significant differences between regions and countries in terms of the percentage of workers who are "informal". In Southern Africa (40.2%) the share of informal employment is less than half that in Central Africa (91.0%), Eastern Africa (91.6%) and Western Africa (92.4%). As Guven and Karlen (2020, n.p.) suggest, in ways that caution against seeing informality as "inherently bad or problematic" (Kanbur, 2021):

The vibrancy of the informal sector is difficult to miss in African cities: street vendors are key in ensuring food security. Those who work in transport keep the city and the economy moving. And those operating in services are critical to the overall incomes and functioning of African cities...and is an important contributor to poverty alleviation.

In this chapter we will suggest that any attempts to understand the contemporary complexities of economic, social, cultural and political development in SSA—including the significance of the informal economy—must be situated, as Kiaga and Leung (2020, p. 7) suggest, in a framework that accounts for the ways in which the "socio-economic political contexts: pre-colonial, colonial, postcolonial and independent Africa shape the conceptualization of formality/informality and its relation to employment". In this context, our provocation—*A New Skills and VET Agenda for SSA?*—will engage with the work of Simon McGrath and colleagues (McGrath et al., 2020) who present a review of the literature on TVET in Africa, and a series of provocations that emerge from that review. At a fundamental level they highlight a concern in much of the research literature that in a context where "formal labour market employment and real wages have been stagnant (as in much of Africa over much of the post-independence period), it is perverse to see the provision of skills as the underlying problem" (McGrath et al., 2020, p. 469).

In *Chapter 5: Central and Eastern Europe (CEE)* we draw on work that suggests that in CEE the informal economy is characterised by, among other things, seasonal migration, part-time employment, a high level of education of employees, trade union structures that are not adapted and do not have experience in how to work with the informal economy, and refugees (Glovackas, 2005, p. 4). In addition:

- Many employees in the formal sector are paid part of their salary informally, meaning no tax is payable on it;
- Informal employment is particularly high in the agricultural sector: in the Republic of Moldova, for example, agriculture accounts for more than 60% of all informal employment;
- Similar numbers of women and men are working informally in most countries in the region;
- Women generally have lower-status jobs than men, despite having similar educational backgrounds. (GIZ, 2019, p. 44)

In this context our provocation will suggest that the challenge is not simply to shift people from informal to formal employment (the "formalisation agenda"). Rather, the challenge is to engage the full range of social partners (including governments, unions, grassroots organisations and education providers) in facilitating lifelong learning arrangements that equip informal workers not only with accredited and certified skills, but also the capacities to participate in (re)shaping new forms of decent work and social protection that are inclusive of people who until now have been caught up in "poverty trap" forms of informal labour.

Our discussion and analysis in *Chapter 6: The Asia–Pacific*, is framed by the social, cultural, economic, political and geographical diversity and complexity of the region. A snapshot of the region's complexity and diversity is captured by the ILO (2018b, pp. 35–38):

- The differences in the size of the informal economy in the region varies considerably with 74.4% of the informal economy in developing Asian countries compared with 21.7% in developed Asian countries.
- Some parts of the region such as Southern Asia (87.8% in 2016) and South-Eastern Asia and the Pacific (75.2% in 2016) have greater shares of the informal economy than Eastern Asia (50.7% in 2016).
- In rural areas, the informal economy contributes to 85.2% of informal employment and is 47.4% in urban areas.
- The scale of the informal economy at a country level varies from 94.3% in Nepal, 93.6% in Lao and 93.1% in Cambodia (highest levels) to below 20% in Japan (lowest level).
- Rates of informal employment in Eastern Asia are higher for men than women, but in Southern Asia, South-East Asia and the Pacific the rates are higher for women than men.
- Young people aged 15–24 account for 86.3% of the informal economy compared to 67.1% of adults aged 25+.
- Most of the workforce (89.7%) in the region with a primary education are in informal employment compared to only 30.7% of the workforce with a tertiary education.

In reviewing and analysing the challenges and opportunities of post-COVID informal economies across the diversity of the Asia–Pacific, our provocation in this chapter acknowledges that opportunities to engage in skill development and LLL are possible, but difficult. Can be limited, but also provide new ways of understanding learning and livelihood trajectories. In other words, a political economy of LLL should seek to acknowledge and identify what this 'promise of LLL' might mean in different contexts, and for different individuals and different groups. And, at the same time, acknowledge and identify why this 'promise' is often 'broken', or remains limited, fragile and precarious.

In our concluding chapter, *Chapter 7: A Political Economy of Informal Working and Lifelong Learning (LLL) for Decent Work and Just Transitions?* we revisit our engagement with the ways in which skills, education and training and contested ideas about Lifelong Learning (LLL) are understood as being central to the problem of "informality", and as the "panacea" to this problem. We review our argument that conceiving of these challenges and opportunities as being structured by a "political economy" of LLL provides a productive avenue to draw on diverse, but critical, theoretical and methodological tools in developing our analysis. The chapter concludes by engaging with the work of McGrath et al. (2020), their identification of a number of emerging trends in VET scholarship in Africa—framed by a focus on *Policy, Systems and Institutions, Vocational Knowledge,* a *Critical Capabilities Approach, VET for Community Development,* and *Skills for Sustainable Development*—and our exploration of how these possibilities might be productive in other postcolonial and development contexts.

References

Alla-Mensah, J., & McGrath, S. (2023). A capability approach to understanding the role of informal apprenticeship in the human development of informal apprentices. *Journal of Vocational Education & Training, 75*(4), 677–696. https://doi.org/10.1080/13636820.2021.1951332

Arab Studies Institute. (2017). *Statement of purpose.* Retrieved 4 June from http://www.politicaleconomyproject.org/

Basto-Aguirre, N., Nieto-Parra, S., & Vázquez-Zamora, J. (2020). *Informality in Latin America in the post COVID-19 era: Towards a more formal 'new normal'?* https://vox.lacea.org/?q=blog/informality_latam_postcovid19

Bauman, Z. (2001). *The individualized society.* Polity Press.

Bauman, Z. (2004). *Wasted lives: Modernity and its outcasts.* Wiley.

Beck, U. (1992). *The risk society.* Polity Press.

Beck, U. (2000). *The brave new world of work.* Polity Press.

Braidotti, R. (2019). *Posthuman knowledge*. Retrieved 24 February from https://www.gsd.harvard.edu/event/rosi-braidotti/

Furlong, A., & Kelly, P. (2005). The Brazilianisation of youth transitions in Australia and the UK? *Australian Journal of Social Issues, 40*(2), 207–225. https://doi.org/10.1002/j.1839-4655.2005.tb00967.x

GIZ. (2019). *Toolkit: Learning and working in the informal economy*. https://www.giz.de/expertise/downloads/giz2019_Toolkit_Informal_Economy_EN.pdf

Glovackas, S. (2005). *The informal economy in Central and Eastern Europe*. https://www.wiego.org/sites/default/files/publications/files/Glovackas-Central-Eastern-Europe.pdf

Guven, M., & Karlen, R. (2020). *Supporting Africa's urban informal sector: Coordinated policies with social protection at the core*. https://blogs.worldbank.org/africacan/supporting-africas-urban-informal-sector-coordinated-policies-social-protection-core

ILO. (2018a). *More than 68 per cent of the employed population in Asia-Pacific are in the informal economy*. International Labour Organisation. Retrieved 22 September from https://www.ilo.org/asia/media-centre/news/WCMS_627585/lang--en/index.htm

ILO. (2018b). *Women and men in the informal economy: A statistical picture*. https://www.ilo.org/global/publications/books/WCMS_626831/lang--en/index.htm

ILO. (2019). *Work for a brighter future: Global commission on the future of work*. International Labour Organisation. https://www.ilo.org/publications/work-brighter-future

ILO. (2021a). *Informal economy in Asia and the Pacific*. International Labour Organization. Retrieved 22 September from https://www.ilo.org/asia/areas/informal-economy/lang--en/index.htm

ILO. (2021b). *World social protection report 2020–22: Social protection at the crossroads—In pursuit of a better future*. https://www.ilo.org/global/publications/books/WCMS_817572/lang--en/index.htm

ILO, UNICEF, & European Training Foundation. (2023). *Enabling success: Supporting youth in MENA in their transition from learning to decent work*. https://www.unicef.org/mena/media/22086/file/Enabling%20Success:.pdf

Kanbur, R. (2021). Introduction: The long discourse on informality as reflected in selected articles of the International Labour Review. *International Labour Review, 160*(1), 1–11. https://doi.org/10.1111/ilr.12227

Kelly, P. (2013). *The self as enterprise: Foucault and the spirit of 21st century capitalism*. Ashgate/Gower.

Kelly, P. (2017). Young people's marginalisation: Unsettling what agency and structure mean after neo-liberalism. In P. Kelly & J. Pike (Eds.), *Neo-liberalism and austerity: The moral economies of young people's health and well-being* (pp. 35–51). Palgrave.

Kelly, P. (2018). Three notes on a political economy of youth. *Journal of Youth Studies, 21*(10), 1283–1304. https://doi.org/10.1080/13676261.2018.1463432

Kelly, P., & Harrison, L. (2009). *Working in Jamie's kitchen: Salvation, passion and young workers.* Palgrave.

Kiaga, A. K. (2020). *The impact of COVID-19 on the informal economy in Africa and the related policy responses.* https://www.ilo.org/africa/information-resources/publications/WCMS_741864/lang--en/index.htm

Kiaga, A. K., & Leung, V. (2020). *The transition from the informal to the formal economy in Africa* (Global Employment Policy Review, Background Paper, Issue). https://www.ilo.org/wcmsp5/groups/public/---ed_emp/documents/publication/wcms_792078.pdf

Klein, N. (2007). *The shock doctrine: The rise of disaster capitalism.* Macmillan.

Lanchester, J. (2015). The robots are coming. *37*(5). Retrieved 29 March, from https://www.lrb.co.uk/the-paper/v37/n05/john-lanchester/the-robots-are-coming

McGrath, S., & Russon, J.-A. (2023). TVET SI: Towards sustainable vocational education and training: Thinking beyond the formal. *Southern African Journal of Environmental Education, 38*(2), 1–18. https://doi.org/10.4314/sajee.v39i.03

McGrath, S., Ramsarup, P., Zeelen, J., Wedekind, V., Allais, S., Lotz-Sisitka, H., Monk, D., Openjuru, G., & Russon, J.-A. (2020). Vocational education and training for African development: A literature review. *Journal of Vocational Education & Training, 72*(4), 465–487. https://doi.org/10.1080/13636820.2019.1679969

Mosco, V. (2009). *The political economy of communication.* Sage.

OECD. (2020a). *COVID-19 in Latin America and the Caribbean: Regional socio-economic Implications and policy priorities.* http://www.oecd.org/coronavirus/policy-responses/covid-19-in-latin-america-and-the-caribbean-regional-socio-economic-implications-and-policy-priorities-93a64fde/

OECD. (2020b). *Informality and employment protection during and beyond COVID-19.* https://www.oecd.org/latin-america/events/lac-ministerial-on-social-inclusion/2020-OECD-LAC-Ministerial-Informality-and-employment-protection-during-and-beyond-COVID-19-background-note.pdf

Ohnsorge, F., & Yu, S. (2022). *The long shadow of informality: Challenges and policies.* World Bank Publications. https://openknowledge.worldbank.org/handle/10986/35782

Palmer, R. (2020). *Lifelong learning in the informal economy: A literature review*. https://www.ilo.org/skills/areas/skills-policies-and-systems/WCMS_741169/lang--en/index.htm

Rifkin, J. (2011). *The third industrial revolution: How lateral power is transforming energy, the economy, and the world*. Palgrave Macmillan.

Safa, O. (2018). *Social development bulletin informality in the Arab region: Another facet of inequality*. https://archive.unescwa.org/sites/www.unescwa.org/files/page_attachments/sdbulletin-informality-arab-region-inequality-final-en.pdf

Sukarieh, M., & Tannock, S. (2015). *Youth rising?: The politics of youth in the global economy*. Routledge.

Sukarieh, M., & Tannock, S. (2016). On the political economy of youth: A comment. *Journal of Youth Studies, 19*(9), 1281–1289. https://doi.org/10.1080/13676261.2016.1206869

Swilling, M. (2020). *The age of sustainability: Just transitions in a complex world*. Taylor & Francis. https://doi.org/10.4324/9780429057823

World Economic Forum. (2020). *The future of jobs report*. https://www3.weforum.org/docs/WEF_Future_of_Jobs_2020.pdf

CHAPTER 2

Latin America and the Caribbean (LAC)

Abstract In this chapter we identify the character and the contours of the informal economy, informal labour market and the challenges for informal workers to engage in meaningful LLL and skills development in LAC. We open the spaces for this discussion by telling a story of Haiti's contemporary social, cultural, economic and political situation, and the possibilities for any real progress in relation to these challenges. We reference the substantial academic and grey literature that suggests that the COVID-19 crisis has amplified the scale, scope and character of the informal economy, indicating that informal employment is the most pervasive "structural weakness" in the LAC economies.

Our provocation argues that the challenges faced by informal workers in the informal economies of LAC are significant and appear not to be amenable to the sorts of remedies that organisations such as the World Bank propose, indeed, the historical actions of many of these organisations have produced these challenges. We examine the influence of the Washington Consensus in shaping the LAC's "lost decade" and the political economy of LLL in LAC.

Keywords Informal economy · Informal workers · Skills development · Political economy · Lifelong Learning · Latin America and the Caribbean · "Disaster capitalism"

Haiti: Ten Years After the 2010 Earthquake and "Workers Live Day by Day"

The World Bank (2023) paints a bleak picture of Haiti's contemporary social, cultural, economic and political situation, and the possibilities, or lack of them, for any real progress in relation to these challenges. Indeed, any attempt to identify these challenges feels much like constructing a litany of disaster, suffering, despair and an almost total lack of hope in what might be done, and by whom, to relieve despair on this scale.

As the World Bank (2023) observes, Haiti's past-present-future "continues to be hindered by political instability, increasing violence, and unprecedented levels of insecurity, which exacerbate fragility". By many measures, Haiti "remains the poorest country in the Latin America and the Caribbean (LAC) region and among the poorest countries in the world". In the context of what it identifies as "the lingering political and institutional crisis, high vulnerability to natural hazards, coupled with violent gangs vying to gain control over business districts", the World Bank (2023, n.p.) indicates that Haiti "had a GDP per capita of US$ 1745.9, and on the United Nations Human Development Index it ranked 163 out of 191 countries in 2022".

These social, economic and political crises are made more complex and challenging because Haiti is "one of the most vulnerable countries worldwide to natural hazards, mainly hurricanes, floods, and earthquakes. More than 96 percent of the population is exposed to these types of shocks" (World Bank, 2023, n.p.). The "litany" we are talking about here includes:

- August 14, 2021, an earthquake measuring magnitude 7.2 on the Richter scale, struck the southern region of Haiti—resulting in 2,246 deaths and 12,763 injured, the destruction of 54,000 houses and 83,770 other buildings, including schools, health facilities and public buildings, a total of US$1.6 billion in damage, and losses of 11% of GDP;
- October 4, 2016 Hurricane Matthew, one of the strongest hurricanes on record, claimed more than 500 lives and caused losses and damages estimated at 13% of the 2015 GDP;
- January 12, 2010 an earthquake of magnitude 7.3 on the Richter scale devastated the capital Port-au-Prince and other parts of Haiti, and killed approximately 250,000 people and wiped out 67% of the country's GDP (Fresnillo, 2020; World Bank, 2023).

Before looking in greater detail at the ongoing consequences made apparent more than a decade after the 2010 earthquake, it is worth noting that the World Bank (2023, n.p.) suggests that climate change processes are "expected to increase the frequency, intensity, and impacts of extreme weather events, and Haiti, while making some progress, still lacks adequate preparedness and resilience-building mechanisms". Crisis and uncertainty pile on despair!

On the ten year anniversary of the 2010 earthquake a number of non-government organisations (NGOs) published commentary on this event and the many challenges and crises that it created, revealed and amplified.

Iolanda Fresnillo (2020), writing for the European Network on Debt and Development (Eurodad)—a "network of 52 civil society organisations (CSOs) from 28 European countries" that campaigns and acts "to ensure that the financial system at the global and European levels is democratically controlled, environmentally sustainable, contributes to poverty eradication and delivers human rights for all" (Eurodad, 2023, n.p.)—highlights the structural social, cultural, economic and political problems that the 2010 earthquake amplified. Fresnillo (2020) catalogues a litany of promises made, and broken, of austerity and neoliberal reform demands made by the International Monetary Fund (IMF), the World Bank and a raft of international aid agencies, of a declining public taxation and revenue base that increased challenges for international debt servicing and public provision of infrastructure, and of entrenched corruption and mismanagement in a largely unregulated economic sector that created numerous opportunities for the breakdown of civil order and the strengthening of criminal gangs.

A decade after the earthquake, more than "30,000 people are still living in camps and 300,000 people live in Canaan, a new informal settlement on the outskirts of Port-au-Prince", "4.6 million Haitians (about 40 per cent of the population) will require urgent humanitarian assistance in 2020, and there are 3.7 million people in acute food insecurity" (Fresnillo, 2020, n.p.). Given these challenges, Fresnillo (2020, n.p.), writing from a perspective that critiques contemporary understandings of debt, debt relief and development argues that "it is clear that much of the progress made through debt relief has already been lost. Haiti's recent history starkly highlights the importance of a new approach to debt crisis prevention and the need for a durable resolution that puts people first. That includes binding global rules on responsible lending and borrowing".

Tula Connell (2020, n.p.), in a commentary article for the Solidarity Center, a US-based, American Federation of Labor and Congress of Industrial Organisations (AFL-CIO) affiliated "international worker rights organization helping workers attain safe and healthy workplaces, family-supporting wages, dignity on the job…greater equity at work and in their community" (Solidarity Center, 2023, n.p.), argues that "workers and their families have not benefited from the billions in international aid that poured into the country after the disaster". As she observes: "Haitians are outraged that the island has received millions of dollars in aid since the 2010 earthquake, but public services and infrastructure are nearly nonfunctional". The economy, "which never recovered after the earthquake and the subsequent cholera outbreak that claimed some 10,000 lives, has worsened over the past three years" (Connell, 2020, n.p.).

In this context of ongoing crisis and despair she cites Reginald Lafontant, secretary general of the Groupement Syndicat des Travailleurs Textil pour la Reimportacion d'assemblage (GOSTTRA), a garment workers union, who claims that "Workers live day by day". Referencing a Solidarity Center report—*The High Cost of Low Wages in Haiti*—that tracked garment workers' living expenses during 2018–2019, Connell (2020, n.p.) claims that more than "60 percent of Haitians survive on less than $2 a day, and more than 2.5 million people fall below the extreme poverty line of $1.23 per day". In addition, the "cost of living in Haiti has increased by 74 percent since the Solidarity Center's first wage assessment in 2014". Faced with these challenges, workers on the current minimum wage "must spend more than half (55 percent) of their take-home pay on work-related transportation and a modest lunch, leaving little else to cover other necessities. Some workers say they can only afford to eat once per day".

In partnership with other members of the Haiti Advocacy Working Group, the Solidarity Center "is calling for policies that focus on an equitable and livable future and 'promote the creation of decent employment that enables Haitian workers to adequately care for themselves and their families" (Connell, 2020, n.p.).

However, this is a hope, and a promise, that seems beyond reach. As we finalise this story in mid-2024, much of Haiti's population continues to be traumatised by a complete breakdown in legitimate governance, and a surge in gang activity and violence centred on Port-au-Prince and its surrounds—which in the first quarter of 2024 had claimed more than 2500 lives (United Nations Security Council, UNSC, 2024).

Introduction

The Latin America and the Caribbean (LAC) region comprises 33 member countries of the United Nations in the region of Latin America and the Caribbean, namely: Antigua and Barbuda, Argentina, Bahamas, Barbados, Belize, Bolivia (Plurinational State of), Brazil, Chile, Colombia, Costa Rica, Cuba, Dominica, Dominican Republic, Ecuador, El Salvador, Grenada, Guatemala, Guyana, Haiti, Honduras, Jamaica, Mexico, Nicaragua, Panama, Paraguay, Peru, Saint Lucia, Saint Kitts and Nevis, Saint Vincent and the Grenadines, Suriname, Trinidad and Tobago, Uruguay and the Bolivarian Republic of Venezuela.

In September 2021, Roxana Maurizio (2021a, n.p.), in a technical note titled *Employment and informality in Latin America and the Caribbean: an insufficient and unequal recovery* for the ILO's Labour Overview Series Latin America and the Caribbean 2021, observed that 18 months on from the start of the COVID-19 pandemic, "the economic, labour, health and social crisis has exacerbated the significant deficits in decent work and the high levels of pre-existing inequality in Latin America and the Caribbean". As Maurizio (2021a, n.p.) indicated, the impacts of the pandemic during that time in LAC were among the most profound around the globe. The evidence of these impacts included: "a previously unseen reduction in the level of economic activity and in employment…a marked deterioration of the productive capacity and closure of enterprises…[and]…a significant contraction in average income and increases in inequality and poverty". In this context, "women, young people, migrants, small- and medium-sized enterprises, and workers with lower qualifications have seen the effects of the crisis most intensely".

More specifically, during 2020, economic activity in LAC contracted by 6.8%, according to the Economic Commission for Latin America and the Caribbean (ECLAC), and 7%, according to estimates by the International Monetary Fund (IMF) (Maurizio, 2021a, p. 8). Maurizio (2021a, p. 8) noted ECLAC's claim that "this is the greatest economic crisis that Latin America and the Caribbean as a whole have experienced in their history since statistical records began in the early twentieth century. During the so-called 'debt crisis', the Gross Domestic Product (GDP) of the region contracted -2.6 per cent in 1983, while the fall in GDP due to international financial turbulence in 2009 was -1.8 per cent".

Importantly for the discussion and analysis that we want to develop in this chapter, within this broad categorisation and calculation of the impacts of the pandemic on economic activity in LAC, there is a "wide range between countries, with relatively minor drops such as those in Paraguay, Guatemala and Nicaragua, and at the other extreme, significant contractions such as those seen in Honduras, Argentina, Peru and Panama" (Maurizio, 2021a, p. 8). Our opening story about Haiti's struggles to recover from a series of natural disasters, and the social, cultural, economic and political turmoil that is entangled with these disasters, a colonial history, and ongoing indebtedness starkly evidence both the diversity of the challenges that many economies in the LAC face, and the particularities and similarities that make these challenges more complex.

In this chapter, our intent is to engage with these issues and challenges in more detail, to identify the character and contours of the informal economy, informal labour market and the challenges for informal workers to engage in meaningful LLL and skills development in LAC. We will reference the substantial academic and grey literature that suggests that the informal sector in LAC was "estimated to represent around half of total employment", and that the COVID-19 crisis has amplified the scale, scope and character of the informal economy, indicating that informal employment is the most pervasive "structural weakness" in the LAC economies (Basto-Aguirre et. al., 2020; OECD, 2020a, 2020b).

Our provocation in this chapter argues that the challenges faced by informal workers in the informal economies of LAC are significant and appear not to be amenable to the sorts of remedies that organisations such as the World Bank propose. We will suggest that the historical actions of many of these organisations have been profoundly implicated in producing the social, cultural, economic and political forces and processes that continue to energise these seemingly "wicked problems". We will explore a number of these concerns via reference to Naomi Klein's (2007) *The Shock Doctrine*, and how her detailed, extensive and highly critical account of the influence of the Chicago School of Economics and the Washington Consensus in shaping the LAC's 'lost decade" can inform a political economy of LLL in LAC.

The Informal Sector and Skills Training in LAC

The LAC region, and the many economies that comprise it are the object of much policy and academic interest and discussion in relation to the many and diverse development challenges the region and its member countries face. As a group of World Bank and academic economists observe in *Employment in Crisis: The Path to Better Jobs in a Post-COVID-19 Latin America*:

> The LAC countries experience macroeconomic fluctuations more frequently and often more severely than most other regions of the world. And crises, not a single crisis, characterize the recent history of most countries in the region. One-third of the fiscal quarters between 1980 and 2018 were periods of crisis in one or more countries in the region. The LAC countries have rebounded from some of these crises, but others have altered their economic trajectories. (Silva et al., 2021, p. 1)

The scale and scope of debates about these recurring and ongoing crises, and their complexity, is beyond the admittedly limited range of our interests here. In this sense, here and in the following section, we want to provide an overview of some of these challenges and the ways in which various regional and international agencies both identify and name these challenges, and provide an outline of what various actors should do to meet them.

In a briefing note for the European Parliamentary Research Service (EPRS), Enrique Gómez Ramírez (2016, p. 2), outlines how in 2013, prior to the pandemic but under the influence of previous crises and disruptions, informal employment "affected 130 million workers" in LAC, including more than 27 million young people, and "represented 46.8% of total non-agricultural employment". This rate of informal employment in non-agricultural sectors "varies from country to country, ranging from 30.7% in Costa Rica to 73.6% in Guatemala. Only sub-Saharan Africa and south and east Asia have higher informality rates".

Various OECD studies suggest that the COVID-19 crisis has amplified the scale, scope and character of the informal economy, indicating that informal employment is the most pervasive 'structural weakness' in the LAC economies (Basto-Aguirre et al., 2020; OECD, 2020a, 2020b). As Basto-Aguirre et al. (2020, n.p.) suggest:

> Both cause and consequence of many of the regions' development traps...informality has been eroding tax collection, undermining productivity growth, and leaving a large share of the workforce vulnerable to shocks for lack of social protection, while feeding on low productivity levels, unsophisticated economic structures, rigid regulations, low skill levels and inefficient institutions.

Picking up on these themes, and referencing various data from multiple OECD studies, Piritta Sorsa and her OECD economist colleagues (2020), provide country-based examples of the impacts of informality on particular populations in the LAC region, including for example:

- Old-age poverty in Colombia is high as low-skilled workers spend much of their working lives in informal employment, without pension contributions;
- In Brazil and Argentina, informal workers retire later than others for the same reason, until they eventually reach the age to benefit from a non-contributory pension;
- In Mexico, poverty and informality are highly correlated among regions.

Sorsa et al. and's (2020, n.p.) particular focus is on identifying those factors implicated in the emergence and maintenance of these conditions, and analysing the impacts of policy responses in various LAC countries over time. From this perspective, informality "tends to keep companies small with often low productivity, as growth would entail high costs of formalisation". Their analysis suggests that, "informal sector productivity in the average LAC country is only between 25% and 75% of total labour productivity, and productivity decreases as informality rises".

Ramirez's (2016, p. 3) briefing note to the EPRS identified that prior to 2016, the "highest rate of informal jobs (49.7%) was among women, compared with 44.5% among men". The majority of "workers aged 15 to 24 (55.7%) also worked in the informal sector, as did 44.9% of those over 25". Significantly, those workers "with the lowest educational level were also more likely to have informal employment: 64.4% of workers with no formal education or primary education, compared with only 26.3% of those with higher education".

Nathalie Basto-Aguirre et al. (2020), from the OECD Development Centre, have suggested that COVID-19 pandemic, and the crises and disruptions that it has produced in LAC "challenges us to rethink social pacts in Latin America, with all actors involved, including civil society, private sector and academics". Referencing work undertaken in the developing economies in the aftermath of the Global Financial Crisis which questioned "*Is informal normal?*" Basto-Aguirre et al. (2020, n.p.) observe that the pandemic, by "revealing the formidable social and economic costs of widespread informality, may be the moment where policymakers, workers and firms start to turn the tide". At the same time, they caution that the "agenda is ambitious and requires a multidimensional perspective where fiscal, labour, and productive transformation aspects must be key ingredients of the rethinking of the social pact in the region".

While the challenges of informality and development in the LAC are formidable, and the "agenda is ambitious", there are numerous examples of the ways in which diverse actors in different settings are attempting to develop responses that are embedded in the opportunities and complexities of these different settings. Robert Palmer's (2020) *Lifelong Learning in the Informal Economy*—a global research and policy literature review conducted for the ILO—identifies a number of examples in LAC that seek to identify the ways in which skills are developed and recognised in the informal sector—and to develop approaches in which formal TVET providers are better able to address the needs of the informal economy.

In Honduras, the *Centros de Educación para el Trabajo* works with low-income rural and urban communities to undertake local needs assessments, and to foster community participation on developing projects that can be linked to the national vocational training institution. In these community-based projects the development of core skills is "combined with gender and literacy training as well as technical and entrepreneurship training" (Palmer, 2020, p. 17). In Mexico the National Institute for Adult Education's *Modelo Educación para la Vida y el Trabajo* (Education Model for Life and Work)—as a "second chance basic and foundation skills training (literacy and numeracy)" project—offers young people and adults the chance to qualify for formal qualifications that can provide pathways to further education and lifelong learning. Integrating basic literacy skills with business and environmental training, the programme allows young people and adults to "obtain officially recognized and accredited 6th and 9th grade qualifications, giving out-of-school individuals a second chance to access education and lifelong learning" (Palmer, 2020, pp. 27–28).

Palmer's (2020, p. 27) review further indicates that in LAC there is evidence of the emergence of a number of non-formal, training-related *active labour market programmes* (ALMPs) that consist of programmes that operate outside the formal education system, and are of short duration (days, weeks, months—rather than years). These ALMPs include such things as:

- second chance basic and foundation skills training (literacy and numeracy);
- technical and vocational skills training, i.e. trade- or job-specific skills training programmes; and
- Core work skills training (e.g. training on communication, critical thinking).

Palmer (2020, p. 27) suggests that for interventions of this type to be appropriate to the diverse circumstances and needs of workers in the informal economy, they need to: "i) be flexible so that they can offer different schemes that fit the informal economy's heterogeneity; ii) offer nationally recognized certification; and iii) provide immediate pay-offs to the participants". In this sense, the more successful training-related ALMPs in low- and middle-income countries, which typically have large informal economies, tend to be multi-skill (offering basic, foundation, technical, vocational and core work skills), multi-setting (classroom and on-the-job) and multi-service (offering support beyond skills training) interventions (Palmer, 2020, p. 29).

Reviewing multiple studies Palmer (2020, p. 29) observes that one of the "key aspects of the youth (jóvenes) programmes in Latin America is the combination of classroom instruction with on-the-job training". One study of "345 training programmes confirmed the benefits of combining classroom training with direct workplace experience", and "impact evaluations of these programmes suggests that it is a promising practice worth emulating". In the Dominican Republic, for example, one such project—*Life skills and employability training for disadvantaged youth*—provided young people with "75 hours of basic or life skills training (mainly work habits and self-esteem), 150 hours of technical or vocational training, followed by a three-month internship in a private firm". Evaluations suggested the project had a "positive impact on transition to formal employment for men (increasing about 17 per cent) and also resulted in a 7 per cent increase in monthly earnings among those employed. These gains are expected to last over time" (Palmer, 2020, p. 30).

Palmer (2020, p. 30) claims that skills-related ALMPs for those working in the informal economy need to be combined with other supporting interventions such as job placement, business development support or improved access to credit. He references the Entra21 programme in Argentina as a skills training intervention targeted at disadvantaged unemployed youth with secondary education. The programme provides "technical and soft skills training in ICT-related activities through in-class learning and internships", and "includes a job placement component and each trainer/implementer is committed to inserting 40 per cent of their graduates into the labour market". Trainees in the programme are provided "with transportation expenses, books, training materials and clothes. Some beneficiaries also receive a monthly stipend". Palmer suggests that in this particular programme, trainees "earnings were 40 per cent higher than non-participants" after completing the course.

Pandemic Recovery and a New Skills and VET Agenda for LAC?

As we indicated earlier, the pandemic—and its associated public health, social, cultural, economic and political crises—amplified the "significant deficits in decent work and the high levels of pre-existing inequality in Latin America and the Caribbean" (Maurizio, 2021a, n.p.). These significant challenges have been canvassed by Roxana Maurizio in a number of recent reports for the ILO, where she has identified particular elements of the economic, labour market/employment, social and policy consequences and challenges emerging as the COVID-19 pandemic wreaked its often deadly disruption to "normal" life in LAC. These consequences and challenges included:

- In 2020, Latin America and the Caribbean saw a contraction in level of economic activity in the order of -7 per cent. This fall is more than double that of the world as a whole and is the largest of all the regions.
- The vast majority of productive sectors dominated by small- and medium-sized enterprises strongly felt the impacts of the crisis. According to ECLAC, no fewer than two million micro- and small enterprises in the region have closed their doors forever.
- Over 26 million people in the region lost their jobs during 2020.
- The negative impacts of the crisis in the region have been significantly greater among women than among men. This was seen, among other indicators, in a greater reduction in female employment (18 per cent) than in male employment (14 per cent) between the first and second quarter of 2020.
- The overview is more complex when age is taken into account alongside gender since it is young women who have experienced the greatest reduction in employment in this crisis.

- Frequently, when formal employment falls, informal employment has a countercyclical role and its level increases. However, in this crisis both formal and informal employment saw pronounced contraction, the latter more intense than the former.
- Further, a significant proportion of independent workers were not included in the exceptions... to distancing and reduced mobility; at the same time, a high proportion of them are self-employed and do not work at home, and for them the possibility of teleworking was limited.
- The intense reduction in informal employment meant that the rate of informality fell (temporarily) in the context of the generalized collapse of demand for employment, particularly in the early months of the pandemic.
- The loss of informal jobs was even more marked for women than for men, due in part to a marked contraction of employment in certain sectors that were hard hit by the crisis (tourism, domestic service), which combine a high rate of informality with feminisation of the jobs.
- The greater exit rates from informal employment led to greater withdrawals from the labour force. (Maurizio, 2021a, pp. 3–5)

In response to these challenges Maurizio (2021b, p. 13) argues that the disruptions and crises amplified by the pandemic make the ILO *Centenary Declaration for the Future of Work* goals to achieve a sustainable future of work with decent work opportunities for all, "even more relevant for achieving a human-centred recovery, especially in a region so ravaged by the pandemic". In her report, *The employment crisis in the pandemic: Towards a human-centred job recovery*, Maurizio (2021b) identifies a number of "priority areas of action" for a "sustainable and human-centred recovery". As she suggests, one of the most significant challenges for the LAC is to "regain a stable path to growth that creates the jobs needed to meet the demand of the increased labour supply". This structural challenge, "has become even more relevant today since it not only involves recovering the significant losses caused by the pandemic but also reversing the economic slowdown that began in the five-year period prior to the crisis" (Maurizio, 2021b, p. 13).

At that time in the midst of the pandemic, Maurizio (2021b, p. 13) argued for the importance of international and government policies "that create the conditions and incentives to sustainably increase exports are central in this context". At the same time she recognised that "in an environment characterized by sluggish global trade, the increase in exports will likely be insufficient to generate virtuous economic development that improves the living conditions of the population". From the institutional spaces that she writes from, Maurizio (2021b, p. 13) suggests that in the circumstances amplified by the pandemic "this requires policies that both promote greater diversification and the incorporation of new exported goods and services, as well as those that boost sectors that supply domestic demand and create jobs, especially for lower-skilled workers". At a general level, this sort of thinking creates a series of demands for:

- strategies that promote sustained increases in productivity and digital transition.
- countries of the region [to] promote the creation of formal employment and the formalization of informal employment through a comprehensive set of instruments.
- measures to support micro, small and medium-sized enterprises (MSME), which have been particularly affected by the crisis.
- [a] just transition agenda has become increasingly relevant and, with it, the measures to guarantee an environmentally sustainable recovery. (Maurizio, 2021b, pp. 13–15)

Against this more general focus on the post-pandemic complexities and challenges of economic development in LAC, Maurizio (2021b, p. 15) shifts her attention to a series of education, training and skills development priorities and challenges that are important for our work here—especially as these priorities emerge from a development economics framework.

Investment in Education and Training

In this context, LAC countries "should increase investment in education and vocational training for current and future jobs. The interruption of face-to-face learning…[revealed]…an evident need to build capacities for digital transformation".

Lifelong Learning

There is a sense here that the "new demands for knowledge and skills that will emerge both during the recovery and in the medium and long-term mean that they must be anticipated and accompanied by efficient, effective systems of lifelong learning that help people to better prepare for transitions in the labour market throughout their working life".

Technological Replacement of Routine Tasks/Jobs

The public health measures of the pandemic—including prolonged periods of shutdown—gave an "impetus" to the use of digital technologies, an impetus that "may be intensifying the existing downward trend in occupations with a high content of routine tasks, as well as promoting the growth of cognitive and non-automated occupations and tasks". In this context, these "processes are accompanied by new knowledge demands, making access to employment even more difficult for certain groups…[indicating that]…new and better strategies are needed for labour policies in the region".

Active Labour Market Programmes

Maurizio (2021b, p. 15) identifies that in the LAC there are a diversity of "active labour market policies with different designs, requirements and target populations, which are implemented from various government spheres, in some cases with the participation of the private sector and enterprises". However, the scale and scope of many of these ALMPs is "insufficient to meet current demands. These programmes often have only a limited impact on the possibility of obtaining formal employment".

Social Protection

Finally, the pandemic "revealed the significant social protection gaps in the region, especially those related to income. In response, countries must advance strategies that guarantee economic security based on universal social protection floors".

Provocation: "Disaster Capitalism" and Elements of a Political Economy of Lifelong Learning in LAC

Any number of researchers and commentators on the challenges that LAC economies and large sections of their populations face have provided analysis and made observations that could inform our provocation here. Our opening story, for example, about the recent, ongoing, litany of disaster, suffering and an almost total lack of hope in what might be done, and by whom, to relieve the despair of the vast majority of Haiti's population included accounts from organisations such as the European Network on Debt and Development and the Solidarity Center working in this space to unsettle the "official" accounts of organisations and agencies such as the World Bank and the IMF about what "ails" Haiti, and what should be done.

Benedicte Bull (2014), for example, explores a political economy of what she calls "weak institutions" and "strong elites" in the so-called Northern Triangle of Central America comprising El Salvador, Guatemala and Honduras. This is an area from which millions of refugees continue to flee from a profound "lack of economic opportunity, environmental challenges, and chronic violence" (Roy & Cheatham, 2023)—and which currently provokes divisive, racially charged partisan political debates about "migrants", "borders" and "criminality" in destination countries such as the US. Diana Roy and Amelia Cheatham (2023) from the US think tank, the Council for Foreign Relations, sketch how in these countries, alongside the environmental disasters (such as hurricanes) exacerbated by climate change, the pandemic amplified the economic crises of the previous four decades—much of which "stem[s] from deep-rooted violence". From this perspective, "decades of civil war and political instability planted the seeds for the complex criminal ecosystem that plagues the region today"—an unstable and complex situation energised by "U.S. interventions during the Cold War". For Bull (2014, p. 125), a political economy of "weak institutions" and "strong elites" in this context is "necessary to get the answers to the core questions of political economy: who has power/resources? How are resources deployed in the pursuit of economic, political and other goals? What are the results? And the most important: how may positive change occur?"

Elsewhere, James Biles (2009), a social geographer, presents a review of various perspectives on the informal economy and informal work in

LAC—"dualist" (formal/informal economy); Neoliberal (informal work is largely a form of entrepreneurial, choice-making economic activity); neo-Marxist (informality as a consequence of globalised capital's production, reproduction and exploitation of workers in contexts that lack a strong state as a counter to exploitation); and poststructuralist (the role of informal work in giving and creating meaning in lives). In this review he seeks some explanation for the continuing significance, size and social, cultural, economic and political consequences of the informal economy and informal labour market in LAC. Taking a longer view of many of these issues, Biles (2009, p. 214) argues that during the so-called lost decade of the 1980s, many of the LAC economies "experienced a profound economic crisis as incomes declined precipitously, inflation skyrocketed, and unemployment increased by nearly 50%". During this "lost decade", "informal work grew more than 30%...accounting for more than 40% of the economically active population by 1990". Biles (2009, p. 214) identifies how, in "response to the economic crisis, the majority of Latin American countries adopted a series of sweeping neoliberal reforms, including trade liberalization, deregulation, and privatization of government-owned enterprises". As he argues, in concert with "currency devaluation and reductions in government spending on social programs and public-sector employment, these structural adjustment programs were imposed at the behest of multilateral financial organizations such as the International Monetary Fund in exchange for access to short-term loans and restructuring of countries' financial obligations" (Biles, 2009, pp. 214–215).

At one level, Biles (2009, p. 215) proposes, somewhat problematically, that "neoliberal reforms have arguably achieved the basic objectives of structural adjustment, as most countries in Latin America have experienced substantial gains in economic growth, trade, and foreign direct investment during the past two decades (although invariably punctuated by periodic economic crises)". The problematic dimension here is that at the same time, "Informal work... has not diminished and...a significant share of men and women from the Río Bravo to Tierra del Fuego remain relegated to precarious, poorly paid work lacking basic social protections and benefits, decent working conditions, a fair wage, and a modicum of job security". Indeed, across LAC "the odds of finding 'decent work' are no better today [2009] than during the economic crisis of the 1980s".

The provocation that we want to sketch here is that the challenges faced by informal workers in the informal economies of LAC are significant, complex and appear not to be amenable to the sorts of remedies that organisations such as the World Bank, the IMF, UNESCO, the OECD, the ILO and international aid and development agencies propose—and which we have outlined. Indeed, the historical actions of many of these organisations and agencies have been directly and profoundly implicated in producing the social, cultural, economic and political forces and processes that continue to energise these seemingly intractable, "wicked problems". Our provocation seeks to explore a number of these concerns via reference to Naomi Klein's (2007) *The Shock Doctrine: The Rise of Disaster Capitalism*, and how her detailed, extensive and highly critical account of the influence of the Chicago School of Economics and the Washington Consensus in shaping the LAC's "lost decade" can inform a political economy of LLL in LAC.

Klein's (2007) work has been influential, productive and provocative. A full engagement and critique of the text, and the commentary about the text, is beyond the scope of the present discussion. However, we want to highlight several key, interconnected features at this time, and think about how these features can carry forward into our final chapter where we bring a number of these threads together: what does Klein mean by the *Shock Doctrine*, where does this doctrine emerge from, and what does it contribute to thinking about a political economy of LLL in LAC?

Klein (2007) situates her concerns and interests in how a series of crises and disasters at the turn of the twenty-first century appeared to make clear, or reveal, a number of forces and intellectual frameworks related to the ways in which the practices and processes of globalising capitalism identified in these disasters moments for extracting value and making extraordinary profits. These disasters included the terror attacks on New York and Washington on September 11, 2001, the "reconstruction" of Iraq after the US invasion of 2003, the destruction wrought on New Orleans by Hurricane Katrina in 2005 and the Indian Ocean tsunami of 2004. In investigating these processes and events, and the ways in which governments, international agencies, global financial institutions and various profit-seekers, thought and talked and acted in relation to these crises, Klein (2007, p. 6) came to identify "these orchestrated raids on the public sphere in the wake of catastrophic events, combined with the treatment of disasters as exciting market opportunities", as "disaster capitalism". Her "genealogy" of these events and the forces at work revolves around a detailed account and analysis of the role played by the radical free-market economist Milton Friedman, the Chicago School of Economics which worked as a laboratory and training ground for the development and spread of Friedman's ideas, and the translation and flow of these economic rationalities into business, government and academia through the 1970s and 1980s in what was to become known, often critically, as *neoliberalism*. Again, the extraordinary detail and breath of Klein's analysis is beyond our scope here. However, her tracing of the development of these rationalities and forces has a significant focus on the impact of Friedman's version of neoliberalism on Chile leading up to and following General Augusto Pinochet's overthrow of the democratically elected government of Salvador Allende in 1973—with, as Klein demonstrates exhaustively, the involvement of United States government agencies such as the CIA, and large US-based multinational corporations. In her analysis Klein (2007, p. 7) argues that not "only were Chileans in a state of shock following Pinochet's violent coup, but the country was also traumatized by severe hyperinflation". In this context, "Friedman advised Pinochet to impose a rapid-fire transformation of the economy—tax cuts, free trade, privatized services, cuts to social spending and deregulation". For Klein (2007, p. 7), the aftermath of the coup witnessed "the most extreme capitalist makeover ever attempted anywhere, and it became known as a 'Chicago School' revolution, since so many of Pinochet's economists had studied under Friedman at the University of Chicago".

As Klein (2007, p. 7) illustrates, Friedman came to refer to this "painful tactic" as "economic 'shock treatment'", and in various contexts in the decades that followed, "whenever governments have imposed sweeping free-market programs, the all at-once shock treatment, or 'shock therapy', has been the method of choice". This "shock therapy" metaphor also has other meanings in the ways in which Kelin develops her analysis—meanings that she identifies as emerging from the CIA's "enhanced interrogation" techniques that were developed and deployed during and after these events. Klein (2007, p. 17) suggests that Pinochet also enabled these "structural adjustments" with "his own shock treatments; these were performed in the regime's many torture cells, inflicted on the writhing bodies of those deemed most likely to stand in the way of the capitalist transformation". In this context, many writers, activists and dissidents in Latin America "saw a direct connection between the economic shocks that impoverished millions and the epidemic of torture that punished hundreds of thousands of people who believed in a different kind of society". Klein (2007, p. 7) cites the Uruguayan writer Eduardo Galeano asking: "How can this inequality be maintained if not through jolts of electric shock?"

Klein (2007, p. 163) demonstrates how these process of "makeover" and "reconstruction" in the lead up to and aftermath of conflict, war and/or economic, social, political and natural disaster and crisis were powerfully shaped in the decades after the 1970s by the work of the Chicago School, and in the development of what has become known as the Washington Consensus—the "colonization of the World Bank and the IMF by the Chicago School". For Klein and others this Consensus consisted of a framework of ideas, rationalities, discourses and policies, "masquerading as technical and uncontentious". As she argues, this Consensus was "made up nothing less than Friedman's neoliberal triumvirate of privatization, deregulation/free trade and drastic cuts to government spending" (Klein, 2007, p. 163). These moments and processes of "shock therapy" have not "always been overtly violent". As Klein (2007, p. 10) meticulously demonstrates throughout her book, in Latin America and Africa and elsewhere during the 1980s, 1990s and beyond, "it was a debt crisis that forced countries to be 'privatized or die,' as one former IMF official put it". In these contexts, in the grips of "hyperinflation and too indebted to say no to demands that came bundled with foreign loans, governments accepted 'shock treatment' on the promise that it would save them from deeper disaster".

The continued use of "shock" and "crisis" as key metaphors by key actors—including the World Bank—in the context of the economic crises amplified by the pandemic is a good indication of the continued power of Klein's analysis. Joana Silva and her colleagues (2021, p. 5), in commentary for the World Bank that is entirely un-self-conscious about the influence of Klein's analysis of the role of the Bank in powering the "litany" of crises visited upon LAC, suggest that large-scale, "macroeconomic shock results in microeconomic reallocation at the worker and firm levels". In such times of crisis, "workers' and firms'" fates are linked. Firms can adjust their "number of employees, hours of work, and wages paid, and workers can choose to accept these offers or search for other options". In this worldview, rational, choice-making actors appear to be unencumbered by the structural inequalities and inequities that characterise informal workers' experiences of informal labour markets. Indeed, crises "can have positive cleansing effects that increase efficiency and productivity" (Silva et al., 2021, p. 8).

In drawing this provocation to a close it is worth considering the cautionary observation of James Biles (2009, p. 233) that, "notwithstanding the influences of globalization and neoliberalism, the majority of people throughout Latin America continue to find meaning in the old saying '*no vivo para trabajar; trabajo para vivir*' (I do not live [merely] to work; I work in order to live life)". With this caution in mind, and what it might mean for thinking about how and why informal workers engage with the exhortations of agencies such as the IMF and World Bank to engage in LLL to develop those skills that would, it is claimed, make their lives less precarious, Biles (2009, p. 233), referencing recent research in LAC, argues for approaches that can "explore and explain how men and women employ informal work in order to mediate the processes of globalization and neoliberalism and, ultimately, find meaning in their daily lives". It is not, in this sense, that LLL and skills development are not valued, or have little place in informal workers "daily lives". It is just that a political economy of LLL in LAC needs to understand and account for the continuing and powerful historical legacies of "shock therapies" and their consequences in different LAC contexts, and to look to different, possibly more radical, ways to think about the possible relationships between skills development, "just transitions" (Swilling, 2020) and the often "broken promise" of "decent work for all" (UNDESA, 2019). We canvas a number of these possibilities in the chapters that follow, and in our final chapter.

References

Basto-Aguirre, N., Nieto-Parra, S., & Vázquez-Zamora, J. (2020). *Informality in Latin America in the post COVID-19 era: Towards a more formal 'new normal'?* https://vox.lacea.org/?q=blog/informality_latam_postcovid19

Biles, J. J. (2009). Informal work in Latin America: Competing perspectives and recent debates. *Geography Compass, 3*(1), 214–236. https://doi.org/10.1111/j.1749-8198.2008.00188.x

Bull, B. (2014). Towards a political economy of weak institutions and strong elites in Central America. *European Review of Latin American and Caribbean Studies/Revista Europea de Estudios Latinoamericanos y del Caribe, 97*, 117–128. http://www.jstor.org/stable/23972443

Connell, T. (2020). *Haiti: Workers still struggle 10 years after earthquake.* Retrieved 25 June from https://www.solidaritycenter.org/haiti-workers-still-struggle-10-years-after-earthquake/

Eurodad. (2023). *Our work, European network on debt and development*. Retrieved 25 June from https://www.eurodad.org/our_work

Fresnillo, F. (2020). *Haiti 10 years after the earthquake: The fight for social and economic justice continues*. Retrieved 10 January from https://www.eurodad.org/10_years_haiti

Klein, N. (2007). *The shock doctrine: The rise of disaster capitalism*. Macmillan.

Maurizio, R. (2021a). *Employment and informality in Latin America and the Caribbean: An insufficient and unequal recovery*. https://www.ilo.org/caribbean/information-resources/publications/WCMS_819029/lang--en/index.htm

Maurizio, R. (2021b). *The employment crisis in the pandemic: Towards a human-centred job recovery*. https://www.ilo.org/sites/default/files/wcmsp5/groups/public/@americas/@ro-lima/documents/publication/wcms_779118.pdf

OECD. (2020a). *COVID-19 in Latin America and the Caribbean: Regional socio-economic implications and policy priorities*. http://www.oecd.org/coronavirus/policy-responses/covid-19-in-latin-america-and-the-caribbean-regional-socio-economic-implications-and-policy-priorities-93a64fde/

OECD. (2020b). *Informality and employment protection during and beyond COVID-19*. https://www.oecd.org/latin-america/events/lac-ministerial-on-social-inclusion/2020-OECD-LAC-Ministerial-Informality-and-employment-protection-during-and-beyond-COVID-19-background-note.pdf

Palmer, R. (2020). *Lifelong learning in the informal economy: A literature review*. https://www.ilo.org/skills/areas/skills-policies-and-systems/WCMS_741169/lang--en/index.htm

Ramírez, E. G. (2016). *Latin America's informal economy: Some formalisation strategies*. https://www.europarl.europa.eu/RegData/etudes/BRIE/2016/589783/EPRS_BRI(2016)589783_EN.pdf

Roy, D., & Cheatham, A. (2023). *Central America's turbulent Northern Triangle*. Council on Foreign Relations. Retrieved 13 July from https://www.cfr.org/backgrounder/central-americas-turbulent-northern-triangle

Silva, J., Sousa, L., Packard, T., & Robertson, R. (2021). *Employment in crisis: The path to better jobs in a post-COVID-19 Latin America*. World Bank Publications.

Solidarity Center. (2023). *Who we are*. Retrieved 25 June from https://www.solidaritycenter.org/who-we-are/

Sorsa, P., Arnold, J., & Garda, P. (2020). *Informality and weak competition: A deadly cocktail for growth and equity in emerging Latin America*. https://voxeu.org/article/informality-and-weak-competition-latin-america

Swilling, M. (2020). *The age of sustainability: Just transitions in a complex world*. Taylor & Francis. https://doi.org/10.4324/9780429057823

UNDESA. (2019). *SDG progress reports 2019: Are we on track to achieve the global goals*. https://www.un.org/development/desa/en/news/sustainable/sdg-progress-reports-2019.html

United Nations Security Council. (2024). *Deadly violence in Haiti at record high, some worst scenarios now realities, special representative tells Security Council, urging deployment of support mission, SC/15674*. Retrieved 22 April from

World Bank. (2023). *Haiti—Overview*. Retrieved 26 October from https://www.worldbank.org/en/country/haiti/overview

CHAPTER 3

The Middle East and North Africa (MENA)

Abstract The chapter begins with a story about Mohammed Bouazizi, a 26-year-old Tunisian street trader who self-immolated in protest over his mistreatment and exploitation by local police and officials. This story opens a window into an overview of challenges and opportunities that characterise the Middle East and North Africa's (MENA) informal economy, informal work, ways in which different populations experience these labour relations and practices and the opportunities that exist, or don't, for engaging in LLL as a means to develop skills that might lead to less precarious forms of work. After reviewing how these issues have been analysed by various international development agencies, the chapter considers examples of skills development programmes for informal workers, to illustrate how participatory, place-based adult and lifelong learning approaches can assist workers in informal employment to develop the skills they need to improve their economic and social conditions. We suggest in our provocation that the skills needs of informal workers in MENA have to be understood in the context of the region's political economy, and the ways that LLL approaches can assist them to adapt to the changing structure and opportunities associated with the Fourth Industrial Revolution as well as ongoing conflicts such as between Israel and Hamas in Gaza.

© The Author(s), under exclusive license to Springer Nature Switzerland AG 2024
S. Brown et al., *Informal Workers and a Political Economy of Lifelong Learning*, https://doi.org/10.1007/978-3-031-72451-0_3

Keywords Informal economy · Informal workers · Skills development · Political economy · Lifelong Learning · Middle East and North Africa · History from below

---

Mohammed Bouazizi: The Story of an Informal Worker Who Ignited a Revolution

On 17 December 2010, Mohammed Bouazizi, a 26-year-old street trader, set himself on fire after being harassed by officials in the central Tunisian town of Sid Bouzid where he made a basic living selling fruits and vegetables. On 4 January 2011, he died from his injuries. The protests that followed his death sparked broad pro-democracy reform protests across the MENA region that became known as the "Arab Spring" (The Editors, 2024). In Tunisia, the protests led to the downfall of the brutally repressive regime of President Zine al-Abidine Ben Ali (Lageman, 2016).

Getting inside the context in which Mohammed Bouazizi lived and worked can help us to unpack what the social historian E. P. Thompson (1968) called the "history from below" of marginalised people taking action to reshape their social and economic conditions in opposition to those who oppress them, and thwart their prospects for making a decent living.

Mohammed Bouazizi's father died when he was only three years old, and by the age of 10 he was doing odd jobs to help the family make an income. He left school before completing secondary education, and when he was a teenager he started selling fruits and vegetables from a cart (The Editors, 2024).

Mohammed sold his produce across the road from the municipal government office building in Sid Bouzid. The area was monitored by local police who were known to harass street traders about not having appropriate licences. Mohammed Bouazizi was regularly bullied by local market inspectors and police officers, who exacted bribes and stole produce from him as an informal "tax" for doing business.

It was these local conditions of oppression and corruption that triggered Mohammed Bouazizi's actions. As Thessa Lageman (2016, n.p.) explained in an article for Al Jazeera that asked *Was the Arab Spring worth dying for?*: "The police had confiscated Mohammed's scales because he refused to pay a bribe. A policewoman allegedly slapped him and insulted his deceased father. When he went to the provincial government to complain, he was not allowed inside the building". Later that day, enraged by the refusal of the governor to respond to his concerns, he returned and set himself on fire outside the local governor's office.

When his cousin, Ali Bouazizi, heard that Mohammed had set himself on fire, he went straight to the local government building to find that Mohammed had been rushed to the local hospital with third degree burns. As protests occurred throughout Sid Bouzid that day, Ali filmed them, and posted a video to Facebook under the title of *The Intifada of the People of Sidi Bouzid*. Ali recalls thinking to himself after his cousin's death that: "Perhaps he thought that he might be better off dead than living under such conditions" (Lageman, 2016, n.p.).

Ali himself was no stranger to resistance to the regime, and this open resistance as a member of an opposition party had thwarted his own economic prospects. As Lageman (2016, n.p.) recounts:

> Ali, who is married with three young children, originally intended to be a lawyer, and graduated from university with a law degree. But because of his activities in the opposition as part of the secular Progressive Democratic Party, he was unable to get a job in his field. Instead, he earns a living from his olive trees, some business in real estate and his supermarket.

If Mohammed Bouazizi came to represent many of the structural injustices associated with unskilled informal labouring in Tunisia, his cousin Ali symbolised the thwarted prospects for university educated opponents of political corruption. Skills alone were no "passport" to a prosperous life in the political economy of Ben Ali's repressive regime.

Mohammed Bouazizi, in ways that he possibly couldn't have imagined as he made a series of fateful decisions that led to his death, assumed heroic status in the cause of pro-democracy opposition to the authoritarian regime of Zine al-Abidine Ben Ali, who had been in power since 1987. By the time of Mohammed's death protests had spread throughout Tunisia. The regime's often violent attempts to suppress the protests drew regional and international condemnation, and provoked further protests and demands, leading, in ways that many could not have dared to imagine, to Ben Ali resigning and fleeing the capital Tunis on January 14 "as demonstrators marched... many of them carrying signs and banners with Bouazizi's image" (The Editors, 2024, n.p.).

Mohammed Bouazizi's heroic status was further confirmed in February 2011 when the main square in Tunis was renamed in his memory. No less significant, his actions led to a reframing of the local trading landscape in his home town of Sid Bouzid:

> Today, the road in Sidi Bouzid that had been called Rue 7 November 1987—after the date Ben Ali seized power—has been renamed Mohammed Bouazizi Avenue. On this same road stands the provincial government building in front of which the fruit vendor set himself aflame. To commemorate his deed, a monument of a stone cart has been erected next to the building, along with a huge image of Mohammed. (Lageman, 2016, n.p.)

By staging his actions in front of that building, in that street, Mohammed Bouazizi made a dramatic, symbolic statement of resistance and opposition to the structural injustices that produce and reproduce the economic lives of informal workers in the MENA region. However, as Lageman (2016) asked a decade ago, and five years after the protests in Tunisia and elsewhere in MENA that were triggered, in part, by Mohammed Bouazizi's death, *Was the Arab Spring worth dying for?*

At the time of Lageman's (2016) story, she reported on what many others have also commented on in terms of the unfulfilled expectations, hopes and aspirations of many of the people of the MENA region. This commentary—which is concerned with exploring the social, cultural, economic and political consequences, complexities, achievements and failures of the diversity of protests that are captured by that umbrella term—is beyond the limits of what we want to do here. However, a sense of some of the disappointments and challenges that existed in 2016 become apparent in listening to Ali Bouazizi's reflections at that time. These reflections need not be understood as facts, but can be engaged with as the emotional affects and intellectual rationalisations of a person deeply impacted by those events who was asked to reflect on them by a journalist.

For Ali, the widespread corruption that was a driver of his cousin's actions, alongside the economics of precarious, informal work, had gotten worse in the 5 years after Ben Ali fled: "Before, only Ben Ali and his family stole and cheated…Now everyone does". Ali Bouazizi told Lageman (2016, n.p.) of "how some Tunisians were 'paying 10,000 Tunisian dinars ($4,900) to land a government job: 'The ones who do this are ashamed, but they say that they don't have any other choice'".

Lageman (2016, n.p.) claims that for many Tunisians, "the only thing that has improved since the revolution is freedom of speech—at least at first". She reports Ali Bouazizi claiming that "These days, you have to once again watch what you say when sitting in a cafe or when posting something on Facebook, especially about subjects such as the army, the police, jihad and Syria".

In 2016 Ali Bouazizi was "no longer active in politics, and did not even vote in the parliamentary and presidential elections last year". Indeed, "I have been too disappointed in all the politicians' broken promises in the last five years". At that time, he argued that the "current ruling party, Nidaa Tounes", was an "extension of the old regime". For Ali Bouazizi, "Ben Ali is in Saudi Arabia, but his people are still here. The system hasn't changed" (Lageman, 2016, n.p.).

When he spoke to Lageman (2016), Ali Bouazizi's activism had shifted to exploring ways to develop social and economic opportunities "through his organisation *Association Al Wafa de Developpement*, which he founded shortly after the revolution". The Association "supports local unemployed people in setting up their own businesses, by providing assistance from international organisations. For instance, someone recently started a small car repair garage, while another launched a business selling rabbit meat" (Lageman, 2016, n.p.).

This development work also includes Ali's involvement "in organising the annual December 17 festival in Sidi Bouzid to commemorate the events of 2010". Lageman (2016, n.p.) reports that "Hundreds of people attended again this year. People waved Tunisian flags and sang the national anthem".

At this time, a protest march also took place, with people carrying signs with the words "Work, freedom, social justice" written large—just as they had five years ago. These days, more and more people in Sidi Bouzid are talking about the need for a second revolution" (Lageman, 2016, n.p.).

Introduction

In this chapter, our intent is to identify the character and the contours of the informal economy, informal labour market and the challenges for informal workers to engage in meaningful LLL and skills development in the Middle East and North Africa (MENA) region, a region that comprises Israel, the Gulf States and the Arab states of North Africa, including Algeria, Bahrain, Egypt, Iran, Iraq, Jordan, Kuwait, Lebanon, Libya, Morocco, Oman, Qatar, Saudi Arabia, Syria, Tunisia, United Arab Emirates and Yemen.

Informal employment in MENA is widespread, and accounts for 68% of total employment—up to 78% in Yemen and 81% in Morocco (OECD, 2021a, p. 1; 2021b). In 2019, 30% of young people aged 15–24 were unemployed or not in school or receiving any training, and for young women the number was as high as 42%. Overall, young people in the MENA region are three times more likely to be unemployed than older workers (ILO et al., 2023).

In a World Bank publication, *The Long Shadow of Informality: Challenges and Policies*, Franziska Ohnsorge and Shu Yu (2022, pp. 225–226) have argued that the main drivers of the informal economy in the MENA region includes limited private sector activity, armed conflict, human capital deficits, low labour productivity and wages and less inclusive growth. A more critical, political economy perspective would suggest that "perhaps the widening share of informal labour in Arab countries in non-agricultural sectors is mainly the result of policies of 'Openness', neo-liberal globalization, youth boom, rural migration in great numbers as a result of neglecting rural areas in general and the agriculture sector in particular, in addition to large waves of incoming migration" (Economic and Social Commission for Western Asia [ESCWA], 2017, p. 2). One of the more recent reports on the challenges and opportunities in the MENA region argues that the underlying issues remain largely unchanged, but point to the need for governments to make greater investments in lifelong learning (ILO et al., 2023).

Building on these often conflicting accounts of the challenges and opportunities in the MENA, the provocation in this chapter argues that the skills needs of informal workers (especially young people) in the MENA region have to be understood in the context of the political economy of the region, and the ways that lifelong learning approaches can assist them to adapt to the changing structure and opportunities associated with the Fourth Industrial Revolution as well as the aftermath of conflicts such as between Israel and Hamas in Gaza.

THE INFORMAL SECTOR AND SKILLS TRAINING IN MENA

In this and the following section, we provide an overview of some challenges and opportunities that characterise the informal economy, informal work, ways in which different populations experience these labour relations and practices, and opportunities that exist, or don't, for engaging in LLL to develop those skills that might lead to less precarious forms of work. In doing this we will discuss how various regional and international agencies both identify and name these challenges, and adumbrate what various actors should do to meet these challenges and opportunities.

The ILO (2024, p. 56), for example, observes that "informal employment has become the norm rather than the exception in most Arab States", and provides several reasons in explaining this. First, the ILO (2024, p. 57) suggests that there has been a series of policy failures in the region, in so far as "macroeconomic, sectoral, industrial and investment policies aimed at facilitating structural transformation in the region have, unfortunately, fallen short in creating decent formal employment within the private sector, especially the manufacturing sector". A compounding factor is that these policies "have tended to emphasize low-productivity growth in construction, tourism and other services sectors, where most of the jobs are informal" (ILO, 2024, p. 57).

A second factor is the lack of regulation and effective enforcement mechanisms around business activity in most Arab states, which have "contributed to high levels of informality, with millions of workers left unprotected" (ILO, 2024, p. 57). Only in Oman have reforms been implemented, in July 2023, to extend social protection to workers in all forms of employment, including migrant workers, most of whom are employed informally (ILO, 2024, pp. 58–59).

A third factor concerns discrimination and racism, and how this affects the vulnerability and precarious employment conditions of MENA's informal workers. Moreover, discrimination, including on the basis of nationality, has driven increased levels of informality among migrant workers and refugees.

> In Lebanon, for instance…[the ILO]…assessed informality and vulnerability among disadvantaged groups, and found that 95 per cent of employed Syrian refugees and 93.9 per cent of employed Palestinian refugees were working informally, compared with 64.3 per cent of the most vulnerable Lebanese population. Compounding these issues are inadequate labour market policies and institutions, along with a shortage of social protection coverage and fragmented social security systems. (ILO, 2024, p. 57)

A fourth factor affecting the extent of informal employment is inequality in education and skills. Analysis by the ILO (2024, p. 58) shows that "for all regions in the world, decreases in levels of informality are strongly related to increases in levels of education". But this is not uniformly the case. The MENA region reveals some anomalies for people with tertiary qualifications:

> In the Arab States, more than 8 in 10 workers with no education were informally employed in 2019. This share decreases with higher levels of education but remains relatively high among those with tertiary education (42.2 per cent). Elevated levels of informality among highly educated workers underscore the insufficient creation of decent and productive jobs in the region, and imply a scarcity of formal, high-value jobs. When individuals with substantial education and expertise are forced into the informal economy, it not only represents a significant underutilization of their talents but also hampers productivity and competitiveness. (ILO, 2024, p. 58)

Interplay between the informal and formal sectors is a feature of MENA's political economy. World Bank researchers Ohnsorge and Yu aver that "informality can provide helpful employment opportunities". However, "where the formal sector suffers from severe distortions and governance is poor, the structural, policy, and institutional causes of informality pose challenges for efforts to diversify economies and reduce reliance on commodity production and the public sector" (Ohnsorge & Yu, 2022, pp. 225–226).

Informal employment did not automatically operate as a "buffer" in the MENA region during the COVID-19 pandemic. The ILO's (2024) most recent *Arab States Employment and Social Outlook - Trends 2024*, for example, showed how, during the pandemic, "the informal economy failed to absorb those who lost their formal jobs", and "the number of informally employed individuals declined by 2 per cent in 2020 compared with 2019". It did, however, serve this buffer function following the initial impact of the pandemic:

> By 2023, informal employment had risen nearly 10 per cent above its pre-pandemic level, while formal employment increased by 6 per cent. In Lebanon, official data indicate that informal employment surged from 54.9 per cent in 2018/19, before the pandemic, to 62.4 per cent in 2022. Similarly, in Iraq, informal employment comprised two thirds of the total employment in the country in 2021. (ILO, 2024, p. 56)

Informal employment is affected by flows of refugees and internally displaced people in the MENA region. Syria is the main source of refugees locally and globally, while Lebanon and Jordan are the main receiving countries "hosting the highest numbers of refugees per capita in the world" (ILO, 2024, p. 11). The ILO reported "a significant number of refugees resort to informal employment, often characterized by unfavourable working conditions" and that besides the difficult humanitarian challenges they experience, "refugees frequently encounter difficulties in the labour markets of their host countries, where they are forced to compete with the local population over jobs" (ILO, 2024, p. 11).

The same is true for internally displaced people (IDPs) who have been forced into migration by conflicts, violence and natural disasters in the MENA region. Countries such as Syria and Yemen and the Occupied Palestinian Territory (OPT) have experienced significant IDP crises which have challenged their resources and infrastructure. This displacement consequently has "triggered economic instability, intensified competition for jobs and housing, and heightened tensions between displaced individuals and host communities" (ILO, 2024, p. 11).

This issue has been worsened by recent events. According to the ILO (2024, p. 55), "the war on Gaza led to significant population displacement, with some 2 million individuals in the Strip forced to relocate, according to the latest figures published by the Palestinian Central Bureau of Statistics". Consequently, "many IDPs have been forced into informal employment with limited job security and substandard working conditions, exacerbating their vulnerability".

Another significant issue often highlighted by international and development agencies concerns the employment, skills and LLL opportunities and challenges associated with the transition from carbon-based to green economies. The ILO has examined this as regards work by the OECD on how the green transition in labour markets "underscores the possibility of deepening existing divides, particularly related to gender, education and skill levels" (ILO, 2024, p. 72). In this context the ILO warns that "marginalised groups" like informal workers, young people, women, migrants, refugees and people with disabilities might be disadvantaged. To address this inequity, it calls for "policy efforts" that will "enhance the participation of these groups in the green economy" (ILO, 2024, p. 72; OECD, 2023).

Several agencies have argued that skills development systems, to be effective in addressing the training needs of informal workers in the MENA region, need to be more closely aligned with labour markets. An African Development Bank Working Paper, for example, emphasised that up-skilling, labour market training and educational reforms "that conform to industry needs will help address the skills mismatches existing in many MENA countries" (Ncube et al., 2014, p. 20).

Achieving this sort of alignment is seen as requiring a multipronged approach. Ncube et al. (2014, p. 20) argue that:

> Addressing the skills mismatch in the short run will require improved training programmes and closer links between tertiary and vocational educational institutions on the one hand, and the private sector on the other. Training programmes should include on-the-job initiatives targeting those already working, as well as graduates with a general education who lack specific work skills. In addition, governments need to develop innovative public-private partnerships and the opportunities for collaboration among large employers, governments and other relevant stakeholders such as higher and vocational educational institutions to transform institutional structures and strengthen the region's economy.

A more recent UNESCO report by Chang and Shehadeh (2020) also describes a multipronged approach that involves MENA governments engaging in dialogue with large employers to link people with jobs through strategic skills planning, skills development and skills matching (Chang & Shehadeh, 2020, p. 7).

This goes to questions of governance. Chang and Shehadeh argue that overcoming skills and labour market mismatches requires governance processes which involve workers and their employers in designing the provision of training. But the limitations of these in MENA are "evidenced by a lack of firm regulations on work-based learning, relevant internship or apprenticeship opportunities aligned to training programmes—making them either obsolete or requiring much improvement before they can serve the demands of the labour market" (2020, p. 7).

Not surprisingly, then, UNESCO emphasises "governance models for TVET should involve relevant local stakeholders and business associations in particular between TVET institutions and the world of work". It argues for Public–Private Partnerships (PPPs) to "enhance the relevance of TVET systems and equip youth and adults with skills needed in the labour market and hence improve levels of employment, decent work, entrepreneurship, and lifelong learning" (Chang & Shehadeh, 2020, p. 7).

But this is not happening in any significant way. In examining the shortcomings of TVET across MENA, the ILO recently highlighted the characteristic features of "successful TVET systems" as including: mechanisms to facilitate regular consultation with private industry councils and labour market information systems; ongoing feedback regarding skills gaps so that topics and training materials can be continually improved; and the provision of flexible practical learning options for students, including internships, apprenticeships and a mix of classroom and workplace-based learning approaches (ILO et al., 2023, p. 40). Against this, the ILO et al. observed:

> TVET systems in most MENA countries, however, have none of these attributes. They use outdated curricula that do not consider the needs of the market, and provide little in the way of hands-on experience. Furthermore, TVET systems are overly centralized in terms of skills planning and budgeting. Centralized decision-making limits local relevance and stifles innovation. It limits the space for TVET centres to engage the private sector to facilitate work experience and job placement. (2023, pp. 40–41)

There are, however, some examples of TVET reform along the lines outlined by the ILO. In Jordan, for instance, in 2021 the government "tried to address the disconnect between its TVET system and the private sector by establishing nine sectoral skills councils, tasked with advising TVET providers on the training and skills needs for each occupation" (ILO et al., 2023, p. 42). And Jordan is not alone. "In Morocco, the Strategy on Vocational Education and Training for 2021 seeks to improve the quality and access to TVET through collaborations and a more coherent approach to stakeholders. The reforms aim to enhance cooperation between TVET institutions and employers to identify the skills required in different parts of the country" (ILO et al., 2023, p. 42).

But these examples belie more general problems with TVET institutions and curricula across the region. For these reasons, the ILO et al. (2023, p. 11) report in 2023 recommended:

> TVET must improve links to the labour market, engage the private sector in skills identification and delivery, and increase workplace learning.

Governments should reduce the social stigma surrounding TVET by building pathways to general education tracks that are supported by National Qualifications Frameworks.

Another theme in reports from international financial institutions is that, if skills development opportunities are to be opened up in the informal sector as well as the formal sector across the MENA region, new approaches to investment in and implementation of training will be required. These new approaches are seen as being necessitated by the widespread nature of informal working conditions in MENA countries which reflect "deep-rooted structural challenges, such as high youth unemployment and bloated public sectors that can no longer absorb additional public servants" (Ohnsorge & Yu, 2022, p. 228). The World Bank and the International Monetary Fund have highlighted the need for "multipronged policies that aim to create a more vibrant private sector, especially to encourage small firms to grow and boost the human capital of workers so that they can be productively employed in a reinvigorated private sector" (Ohnsorge & Yu, 2022, p. 228). Researchers in these international financial institutions not surprisingly call for fiscal reform in the region. This includes "reducing excessive corporate tax burdens and enhancing revenue collection through harmonized electronic filing systems (for example, Morocco) or the introduction of a value-added tax (for example, Egypt)" (Ohnsorge & Yu, 2022, p. 226). In addition, "policies to promote entrepreneurial activities, such as easing of business licensing requirements, can also facilitate entry of informal workers into more productive jobs in the formal sector" (Ohnsorge & Yu, 2022, p. 227).

UNESCO researchers recommend greater policy attention be placed specifically on developing TVET programmes aimed at assisting informal workers and businesses. However, in the MENA region "developing policies and taking measures as required by TVET sector institutions to organise informal apprenticeships in informal sectors of the economy…currently lies outside the field of interest of mainstream government activity in the TVET sector" (Chang & Shehadeh, 2020, p. 71). This suggests that government institutions in MENA need to take a stronger interest in seeing TVET as an investment in shaping the skills required for capturing economic development opportunities as well as creating more inclusive societies.

The World Bank suggests governments could work with the private sector to improve the access of MENA firms to finance by, among other things, strengthening legal frameworks and improving credit protection arrangements (Ohnsorge & Yu, 2022, p. 229). Doing so, according to these prescriptions "can promote formal private sector activity by increasing the transparency of firms to investors and facilitating investment" (Ohnsorge & Yu, 2022, p. 229). Furthermore, "adoption of financial technologies (fintech), such as innovations that automate financial transactions, can also facilitate access to financial services by informal unbanked individuals and SMEs" (Ohnsorge & Yu, 2022, p. 229). These approaches are seen as helping informal workers and SMEs to engage more effectively in entrepreneurial activities and shape decent work opportunities (including skills development and access to training) for themselves and their workers.

The World Bank also underlines the importance of using public–private partnerships (PPPs) to improve investment in human capital. It prescribes government policies that expand job training to help MENA's young people enter formal and more productive jobs. Similarly, training programmes are seen as helping women to increase their mobility, especially where they are combined with training in both hard and soft skills (Ohnsorge & Yu, 2022, p. 230).

Pathways to Social and Economic Justice for Informal Workers: Partnerships for Creating Local Learning and Skills Development

The Deutsche Gesellschaft für Internationale Zusammenarbeit (GIZ) is Germany's primary development agency, and is part of the German Federal Ministry for Economic Cooperation and Development (BMZ). The GIZ *Toolkit: Learning and working in the informal economy* (2019) describes a partnership project in Palestine that adapted the education and training system to better meet the needs of the labour market and young people. 15 NGOs in the West Bank, Gaza Strip and East Jerusalem provided non-formal adult training, in particular for disadvantaged target groups as a means of combating poverty and conducting labour market analyses. The courses were developed and implemented with the target groups, and partnerships for employment were created. It was mainly funded by the European Union for three years (2012–2014).

The programme empowered young people to generate income in informal or formal labour markets. Teaching staff used participatory learning methods to integrate widely differing groups of people into learning experiences and help school dropouts rediscover the joy of learning. Around 1,800 people participated, and a study undertaken 6 months after completion showed about 40% of participants found a job or started their own business with their newly acquired knowledge and skills.

NGOs received support to help course participants gain a foothold in the labour market. This included internships and visits to potential workplaces, forwarding to job exchanges, microfinance institutions or other actors who provided advice and financial support for business start-ups. Ten of the NGOs set up local educational partnerships to help disadvantaged groups access continuing education (GIZ, 2019, pp. 145–146). In our Provocation, we will return to identifying several challenges that the ongoing conflict between Israel and Palestinian groups have for such initiatives.

Another example of skills development programmes for informal workers in the region is one successfully piloted in Jordan jointly by the ILO and the International Youth Foundation to upgrade informal apprenticeships. This pilot aimed at: developing the apprenticeship model and process; linking apprentices with employers for on-the-job training; improving workplace occupational health and safety conditions; improving work organisation and workplace management; and organising testing for occupational licences for apprentices. It involved six months of basic training followed by three to five months of on-the-job training. After completing the basic training, each participant was assigned to a garage as an apprentice. During on-the-job training, apprentices received transportation allowance, insurance against work-related injuries and a work uniform. A summary of this innovative programme's outcomes underscores its effectiveness: 75% of participants completed it; 92% of apprentices obtained a job; and 90% secured better than the minimum wage (Palmer, 2020). As Palmer remarks:

> Compared to traditional informal apprenticeships, this pilot shortened the transition period from apprentice to employed skilled worker with less than one year of training as opposed to up to five years in a typical apprenticeship. (Palmer, 2020, p. 26)

Examples like these illustrate how participatory, place-based adult and lifelong learning approaches can assist informal workers to develop the skills they need to improve their economic and social conditions. Equally, they highlight the roles that international development agencies and national governments can play in stimulating economic activity and creating skills development opportunities for vulnerable workers as well as small and micro enterprises in post-conflict settings such as Gaza.

A feature of the global political economy is the impact of fast-paced technological change. The ILO has factored this into its analysis of the challenges and opportunities associated with skills development in MENA:

> Collectively referred to as the fourth industrial revolution, increased digitalization, automation and use of artificial intelligence is changing how people live, communicate and work. Technological innovation can be an engine of economic growth and job creation, offering new possibilities in education, communication, and productivity. But it can also exacerbate wage inequality and displace workers. Around 45 per cent of work activities in MENA could potentially be automated in sectors as diverse as manufacturing, transportation, construction, hospitality, and retail. At the same time, technological innovation can improve lives and livelihoods, making it easier for people to learn and work across borders and boundaries, without necessarily having to leave their own countries. (ILO et al., 2023, p. 71)

Education and training systems in MENA, however, have not adapted to these complex and, in many ways, harsh realities associated with a global capitalism. These transformations could result in nearly half of the work roles in the MENA region being automated, and workers becoming "supernumerary", of "no use" on the margins of global capitalism (Bauman, 2004, pp. 5–7).

In this context, informal workers require access to training in not only technical skills but also transferable skills which enable them to succeed in transitioning between new jobs as they emerge. Beyond technological skills, workers increasingly need complex problem-solving (creativity and collaboration), and soft skills (leadership, communication and curiosity) (ILO et al., 2023, p. 71). The necessary systemic transformation of education systems required is spelled out by the ILO et al. (2023, p. 71):

> To benefit from the opportunities presented by the fourth industrial revolution, MENA countries will need to introduce more adaptive education

systems. They will need to evolve and adapt quickly to changing market environments and opportunities, and be flexible enough to embrace and support different learning styles, rather than forging students into the same uniform mould. Necessary steps will include building the IT skills of teachers and trainers, integrating IT skills throughout the education curricula, creating more space for critical thinking and problem-solving, providing teachers with the necessary training and autonomy to pursue differentiated learning and devoting more resources to lifelong learning.

Lifelong learning capability will be a critical enabler in positioning people to operate successfully in these new economic and social realities—globally and in the MENA region. This requirement for adaptive skills has been well captured in the ILO's *Enabling Success: Supporting Youth in MENA in their Transition from Learning to Decent Work* report:

> In the digital era, advances in technology call for new skills seemingly overnight. It has become more difficult to anticipate which job-specific skills will be required next. This uncertainty places a premium on essential life skills that enable people to adapt quickly to changing circumstances. An emphasis on lifelong learning, and an ability to unlearn and relearn, will become especially important. This is worrisome in a region where educational institutions focus exclusively on teaching to the curriculum and where students rarely take the initiative to search for knowledge outside the classroom. (ILO et al., 2023, p. 25)

Access to educational opportunities in the digital era are particularly problematic in a region where internet access is far from universal. The ILO et al. (2023, p. 32) recently observed this in relation to the impact of the COVID-19 pandemic on the MENA region's educational disadvantage:

> The COVID-19 pandemic exposed the MENA region's vulnerabilities and exacerbated its challenges…Once schools were forced to close, the region's digitalization gap became obvious, as remote-learning mechanisms were lacking in many communities. While some countries switched to remote learning, others lacked capacity…In 2020, it was estimated that 40 per cent of the region's students across all educational levels did not benefit from any remote learning initiative.

There are relatively few examples of the use of internet-enabled technologies being used in MENA to deliver vocational learning in the informal economy along the lines described in other regions. Palmer (2020) cites some emerging examples of how new technologies are providing early adopters in some regions, including MENA, with new learning opportunities. For example, in informal agriculture, apps are helping workers to enhance their numeracy skills and apply better farming practices.

In Tunisia an app available via the Tunisian Public Employment Service is being used to teach soft skills and job search skills (Palmer, 2020, p. 35).

Addressing the digitalisation gap, and transforming the TVET system so it provides more equitable access for young people including informal workers to the skills training they need to succeed in the Fourth Industrial Revolution context will require greater investment in the region's TVET systems. In MENA the TVET system is currently financed through a variety of means:

- Student fees: secondary TVET education is generally free of charge;
- Budget allocations: even though TVET funding is still comparatively low, it has increased in the recent years;
- Donors and international partners, including the EU, World Bank and governments such as Canada, France, Germany and the United States. (Chang & Shehadeh, 2020, p. 21)

Chang and Shehadeh (2020, p. 22) call for more investment and funding to enhance institutionalised partnerships between TVET institutions and the world of work. While these represent an attractive option for co-financing skills development initiatives with informal workers, they are not without their challenges in MENA countries. As the majority of TVET providers are in the region's large public sector, with its associated large expenditures on wages, a key challenge concerns the inadequacy of resources for meeting development expenses and investments in reform initiatives, such as teaching and learning materials, equipment and infrastructure enhancement.

PROVOCATION: A POLITICAL ECONOMY OF LIFELONG LEARNING (LLL) IN THE CONTEXT OF CONFLICT AND DIGITAL REVOLUTIONS

The skills needs of informal workers (especially young people) in MENA have to be situated and understood in the context of the region's political economy. Particularly in relation to how LLL approaches can assist them to adapt to the changing structure and opportunities associated with the Fourth Industrial Revolution, as well as the aftermath of conflicts such as between Israel and Hamas in Gaza. This is an important consideration, given that, "MENA governments have been unable to fundamentally transform the region's political economy in order to stimulate job creation" (ILO et al., 2023, p. 68).

For example, many of the employment and skills related gains made in Gaza during recent decades will have been diminished or wholly negated by the Israel-Hamas war in Gaza that has been raging since October 7, 2023. A recent ILO Brief (2023, p. 4) on the situation paints a stark picture of the Gazan political economy:

> The Israel-Hamas conflict is resulting in a deep humanitarian crisis in Gaza, with huge implications on the labour market, employment prospects and livelihoods, not only within Gaza, but also in the West Bank. Entire neighbourhoods in Gaza have been destroyed, there has been widespread damage to infrastructure, businesses have closed, large-scale internal displacement has occurred, and the lack of water, food and fuel are severely crippling economic activity. While the impacts on jobs and livelihoods in Gaza are undoubtedly huge, a quantitative assessment in this early stage of the conflict must rely on estimates and projections, as opposed to primary data.

The ILO (2023, p. 6) sees itself playing a significant role in the post-conflict reconstruction and recovery of Gaza and the West Bank, in ways that will contribute to skills development for workers whose employment and livelihood prospects have been severely affected by the conflict:

> Once the situation allows, the focus should shift towards recovery and reconstruction efforts. The ILO's Employment Intensive Infrastructure Programmes can be pivotal in this context. These public works programmes not only contribute to the rebuilding of infrastructure and the repair of damaged assets but also provide emergency employment opportunities for the local workforce, all within the framework of decent work. These schemes can also be coupled with skills development programmes, which will be vital in the recovery process.

Investment in educational infrastructure will also be important in the recovery of economies and societies affected by conflict, such as in Gaza and the West Bank. So too will grants by governments and international development agencies to support affected employers to provide employment and training opportunities to workers in the region. The

ILO (2023, p. 6) suggests this could take the form of income support and wage subsidies, as these can help businesses retain existing workers as well as take on new ones. In addition, grants that target "self-employed individuals, social and solidarity economic units, micro and small enterprises, and those operating in the informal sector" will be an important part of the policy mix in rebuilding and reshaping the region's political economy. This will also be important in terms of people's capacities to intervene in and transform the political and economic structures that have created vulnerability and exclusion for so many from decent work and livelihoods.

Some researchers on the informal economy in MENA have argued that the solution for the region does not necessarily lie simply in formalising the informal sector and that governments need to devise new approaches (Economic and Social Commission for Western Asia [ESCWA], 2017, p. 7). Any such approaches should include involving informal workers in more inclusive and participatory policy-making processes—a shift towards a *nothing about us without us* approach to shaping policies and programmes to improve the economic and social circumstances of informal workers. This argument has been made strongly, for example, by Chen and Harvey when they called for "a more inclusive approach to the informal economy in the MENA region":

> If labor markets in the region remain rigid and segmented, with a formal workforce that receives social protections and economic benefits that are denied to the unemployed and the informally employed, frustrations could again erupt in social unrest. It is critical for governments in the region to not only pursue employment-led growth, but also to reverse the previous social contract that created a sense of social and economic exclusion among the working poor in the informal economy. This could include measures to increase and expand social protections, adopt inclusive approaches to city and economic planning, and create platforms for informal workers to exercise voice and influence over the policy-making and rule-setting processes that affect their lives. (2017, p. 34)

A more inclusive approach would entail the involvement of informal workers in co-designing the possibilities for effecting change in their circumstances and prospects, including the development of the skills they require in current global and local contexts. Such an approach would recognise that the various elements of the MENA region's political economy range from more formalised international and national institutions of political power and policy-making, through to the workings of private sector businesses (at national and transnational scale), and to place-based community institutions, traditions, workspaces and networks of social, economic and cultural activity. Here, Ali Bouazizi's organisation, *Association Al Wafa de Développement*, and its support of "local unemployed people in setting up their own businesses, by providing assistance from international organisations" (Lageman, 2016) offers a productive example in the aftermath of Tunisia's role in the Arab Spring.

Imaginings of more inclusive and participatory policy-making, and establishing platforms to enable workers to exercise voice and influence, can be informed by the sorts of perspectives associated with E. P. Thompson's (1968) "history from below", and his focus on understanding how disadvantaged and marginalised people can, and must, participate in the re-making of their economic and social circumstances. Mohammed Bouazizi, his cousin Ali and the many others who have resisted, and who continue to "resist", the authorities and forces and relations that oppress them, give expression to what E. P Thompson describes as class consciousness—not as a conceptual matter but as something that happens in particular socio-political circumstances. As Thompson explained in his work on the *Making of the English Working Class* (1968, pp. 8–9):

> class happens when some men, as a result of common experiences (inherited or shared), feel and articulate the identity of their interests as between themselves, and as against other men whose interests are different from (and usually opposed to) theirs. The class experience is largely determined by the productive relations into which men are born—or enter involuntarily. Class-consciousness is the way in which these experiences are handled in cultural terms: embodied in traditions, value-systems, ideas, and institutional forms. If the experience appears as determined, class-consciousness does not. We can see a logic in the responses of similar occupational groups undergoing similar experiences, but we cannot predicate any law. Consciousness of class arises in the same way in different times and places, but never in just the same way.

In considering the challenges experienced by informal workers in the MENA region, and their need to develop skills that enable them to find, participate in and secure "decent work" it is vital to consider, analyse and support how they understand, express and seek to shape their own circumstances and options. Taking this approach, we argue, is part of the challenge, and opportunity, in shaping a political economy of LLL for and with informal workers in the MENA region to foster decent work and "just transitions" for these people (Swilling, 2020).

References

Bauman, Z. (2004). *Wasted lives: Modernity and its outcasts*. Wiley.

Chang, D., & Shehadeh, S. (2020). *Enhancing institutionalized partnerships between TVET institutions and the world of work in the Arab region*. https://policycommons.net/artifacts/8215634/enhancing-institutionalized-partnerships-between-tvet-institutions-and-the-world-of-work-in-the-arab-region/9128189/

Chen, M., & Harvey, J. (2017). *The informal economy in Arab nations: A comparative perspective*. https://www.wiego.org/sites/default/files/migrated/resources/files/Informal-Economy-Arab-Countries-2017.pdf

Economic and Social Commission for Western Asia, ESCWA. (2017). *Informality in the Arab region: Another facet of inequality*. https://archive.unescwa.org/sites/www.unescwa.org/files/page_attachments/sdbulletin-informality-arab-region-advance-copy-en_0.pdf

GIZ. (2019). *Toolkit: Learning and working in the informal economy*. https://www.giz.de/expertise/downloads/giz2019_Toolkit_Informal_Economy_EN.pdf

ILO. (2023). *Impact of the Israel-Hamas conflict on the labour market and livelihoods in the Occupied Palestinian Territory*. https://www.ilo.org/publications/impact-israel-hamas-conflict-labour-market-and-livelihoods-occupied

ILO. (2024). *Arab states employment and social outlook—Trends 2024, promoting social justice through a just transition*. https://www.ilo.org/publications/major-publications/arab-states-employment-and-social-outlook-trends-2024-promoting-social

ILO, UNICEF, & European Training Foundation. (2023). *Enabling success: Supporting youth in MENA in their transition from learning to decent work*. https://www.unicef.org/mena/media/22086/file/Enabling%20Success:.pdf

Lageman, T. (2016, January 3). *Mohamed Bouazizi: Was the Arab Spring worth dying for? Five years since the Tunisian fruit vendor died after setting himself on fire, his family still hopes for change*. Al Jazeera. Retrieved 26 February from https://www.aljazeera.com/news/2016/1/3/mohamed-bouazizi-was-the-arab-spring-worth-dying-for

Ncube, M., Anyanwu, J. C., & Hausken, K. (2014). Inequality, economic growth and poverty in the Middle East and North Africa (MENA). *African Development Review, 26*(3), 435–453. https://doi.org/10.1111/1467-8268.12103

OECD. (2021a). *MENA-OECD government business summit—Session 4. Social resilience: Moving away from informality to formal employment and businesses*.

https://www.oecd-events.org/mena-oecd-government-business-summit/en/session/299dda56-0583-eb11-b566-000d3a20ecf5/social-resilience-moving-away-from-informality-to-formal-employment-and-businesses

OECD. (2021b). *Session 4. Social resilience: Moving away from informality to formal employment and businesses* (MENA-OECD Government Business Summit, Issue). https://www.oecd.org/mena/competitiveness/issue-paper-session-4.pdf

OECD. (2023). *Job creation and local economic development 2023: Bridging the great green divide.* https://www.oecd-ilibrary.org/employment/job-creation-and-local-economic-development-2023_21db61c1-en

Ohnsorge, F., & Yu, S. (2022). *The long shadow of informality: Challenges and policies.* World Bank Publications. https://openknowledge.worldbank.org/handle/10986/35782

Palmer, R. (2020). *Lifelong learning in the informal economy: A literature review.* https://www.ilo.org/skills/areas/skills-policies-and-systems/WCMS_741169/lang--en/index.htm

Swilling, M. (2020). The age of sustainability: Just transitions in a complex world. *Taylor & Francis.* https://doi.org/10.4324/9780429057823

The Editors. (2024, May 6). *Mohamed Bouaziz Tunisian street vendor and protester.* Britannica. Retrieved 1 July from https://www.britannica.com/biography/Mohamed-Bouazizi

Thompson, E. P. (1968). *The making of the English working class.* Pelican Books.

CHAPTER 4

Sub-Saharan Africa (SSA)

Abstract The chapter begins with a story about blood diamonds that illustrates how a continent such as Africa, rich and abundant in natural resources, continues to struggle with forms of exploitation, a lack of transparency with global supply chains, often dangerous and largely unregulated labour practices, inequities and widespread poverty. This story captures some of the complexities of informal work, issues of exploitation and extraction and the limits as well as possibilities of a political economy of LLL in Sub-Saharan Africa (SSA). It opens a discussion on the issues for workers in informal employment and the challenges in achieving the goal of creating decent work for all. In doing this, we describe some of the shifting and complex relationships between the informal and formal economy in SSA that recognise formal workers at the expense of informal workers. We explain how international organisations are working together to develop and implement multiple agendas to create a more prosperous and sustainable Africa. In our provocation we draw on critical analyses of technical and vocational education and training (TVET) in SSA to argue for a need to prioritise concepts such as sustainability and just transitions, if we are to counter TVET's complicity in the Capitalocene and extractivism.

Keywords Informal economy · Informal workers · Skills development · Political economy · Lifelong Learning · Sub-Saharan Africa · Sustainability · Capitalocene

Blood Diamonds: The Informal Economy of Mining in Sub-Saharan Africa

In a recent *Time* magazine article, Aryn Baker (2024) traces the inequities, forms of exploitation, global supply chains, lack of transparency—in spite of international agreements and treaties—and the precarious, often dangerous and largely unregulated labour practices that characterise the mining in Sub-Saharan Africa of so-called conflict or blood diamonds, those diamonds sourced from war zones, contributing to conflicts, and funding armed groups or rebellions.

The power of Baker's investigation, given the great deal that is already known about the mining, export and sale of these diamonds, lies in several of the stories that he tells of the circumstances, conditions, costs and very few benefits, which characterise the experience of the millions of miners working in these conditions.

Mbuyi Mwanza, for example, is identified by Baker (2024, n.p.) as "a 15-year-old who spends his days shoveling and sifting gravel in small artisanal mines in southwest Democratic Republic of Congo" (DRC). Mining work, for Mbuyi and the other miners (young and old), is "grueling, and he is plagued by backaches, but that is nothing compared with the pain of seeing his family go hungry. His father is blind; his mother abandoned them several years ago". In these circumstances Mbuyi has not found a diamond for 3 months, and "his debts—for food, for medicine for his father—are piling up. A large stone, maybe a carat, could earn him $100, he says, enough to let him dream about going back to school, after dropping out at 12 to go to the mines—the only work available in his small village". Mbuyi claims to know "of at least a dozen other boys from his community who have been forced to work in the mines to survive".

The mine where Mbuyi works—"a ruddy gash on the banks of a small stream whose waters will eventually reach the Congo River"—is, according to Baker (2024, n.p.), typical of these sorts of mine in that it is "at the center of one of the world's most important sources of gem-quality diamonds. Yet the provincial capital, Tshikapa, betrays nothing of the wealth that lies beneath the ground". In Tshikapa, in the Kasai Province in the DRC, "none of the roads are paved, not even the airport runway". In settings such as this, "hundreds of miners die every year in tunnel collapses that are seldom reported because they happen so often", and teachers at "government schools demand payment from students to supplement their meager salaries". As a consequence of these processes of extraction and exploitation that produce little in the form of income and resources for local communities, "parents choose to send their teenagers to the mines instead". According to Mbuyi, "we do this work so we can find something that will let us eat...when I find a stone, I eat. There is no money left for school".

Africa, renowned for being the most abundant continent in natural resources, continues to grapple with widespread poverty, prompting the question: where is Africa's wealth flowing? (Patel, 2018). To contextualise Africa's poverty challenge, in 2018 Sub-Saharan Africa faced an average poverty rate of around 41%, with 27 of the world's 28 poorest countries located in this region (Patel, 2018). Despite some progress, the COVID-19 pandemic has impeded advancements, leading to regression in poverty levels in many instances (United Nations Conference on Trade and Development, 2021).

The mining, export and sale of "blood" diamonds is worth more than $US80 billion on an annual basis, yet their extraction and trade are characterised by stark disparities in where this wealth flows in interconnected, global trade networks and alliances (Laube-Alvarez, 2022). The "blood" diamond supply chain witnesses 65% of global diamond production originating from Africa. Despite diamonds being synonymous with luxury, the extraction process reveals, as Mbuyi's story illustrates, a starkly unglamourous reality marked by multiple forms of human rights violations including child labour (Baker, 2024; Kippenberg, 2018). The conditions in diamond mines often involve appalling work environments, labour-intensive and dangerous tasks, meagre wages, managerial violence and adverse effects on local communities.

The analysis of the "blood" diamond supply chain begins with the miners, who often receive minimal pay, whether they are adults or children. Nearly a million African miners earn less than $1 per day (Benaicha, 2021). The industry comprises two primary types of mines: industrial mines and artisanal/small-scale mines. Artisanal mining, which is less formal and regulated, poses challenges in cracking down on illegal operations and enforcing measures to address human rights and working condition violations (Amnesty International, 2013).

As the diamonds progress through the supply chain, crossing borders and undergoing various stages of development, transparency diminishes. Mining operations feed into traders in trading hubs in Belgium and the United Arab Emirates (UAE). In 2021, the UAE surpassed Belgium as the leading rough diamond trading hub, trading $22.8 billion of rough diamonds (Barrington, 2022).

The making of these massive profits on the backs, and with the blood, of largely unregulated mine workers afforded little protection by the governments where these diamonds are mined, and/or the key players in their mining and trade (often militias or criminal gangs, global companies and diamond traders in diamond markets and supply chains) has created demands for the international market to enforce regulations, and promote transparency and ethical sourcing. The European Commission (2024) claims that these demands are achieving little for the miners currently working, and/or the migrants who, historically, worked in the mines under dangerous and degrading conditions, and who were not fairly compensated for their work.

The "blood" diamond mining industry is also characterised by large numbers of migrant workers seeking better opportunities than in their countries of origin. More than half of the individuals who migrate internationally are engaged in migrant labour. Despite the potential advantages of secure and regular labour for both migrants and employers, migrant workers still encounter significant vulnerabilities in their workplace. For numerous migrant mineworkers, these vulnerabilities extend beyond difficulties in their work environment, encompassing broader systemic challenges. Many reside in congested "hostels" alongside their colleagues, enduring limited ventilation. Separated from their families for extended periods, they face not only the physical hardships of their living and working conditions but also increased susceptibility to diseases such as tuberculosis, silicosis and HIV (European Commission, 2024).

Additionally, large numbers of migrant mineworkers struggle to access earned social benefits and programmes, including pensions, compensation and crucial reintegration support (European Commission, 2024). The European Commission cite the example of Moises, a former migrant mineworker from Mozambique, who returned to his home country and developed an initiative to reform the system of exploitative, informal labour. Having faced difficulties accessing pension funds he contributed to during his years of work in South African mines, Moises committed himself to assisting fellow migrant mineworkers in asserting their employment rights. Alongside colleagues, he established the Association of Mozambican Mineworkers (AMMO) to educate others about their rights, and how to access available support services. They also engaged in advocacy efforts with various stakeholders to alter the mechanisms that prevented individuals and communities in their countries of origin from benefiting from the labour of mineworkers abroad (European Commission, 2024).

Moises emphasised the positive impact of migration on educating children and the substantial role migrant remittances play in the country's GDP. The Mainstreaming Migration into International Cooperation and Development (MICD) project, funded by the EU and operational from 2017 to 2021, sought to enhance the integration of migration into international cooperation and development policies. This initiative aligned with the imperative of upholding migrant workers' rights in order to facilitate meeting key Sustainable Development Goal (SDG) targets (European Commission, 2024). The MICD project provided a powerful example of how employment interventions can consider migration aspects to enhance development outcomes. As part of the initiative the Voices from the Underground project shared the work of AMMO through enhanced knowledge, organisational, and technical capacities (European Commission, 2024). The project comprised three key components:

- Institutional capacity-building for the AMMO.
- Facilitating legal services and counselling for mine workers and their families in collaboration with Lawyers for Human Rights (LHR).
- Advocacy and communications at national and regional levels to foster dialogue with stakeholders and inform beneficiaries of their rights. (European Commission, 2024)

The European Commission (2024) argue that migrant workers have the potential to significantly contribute to sustainable development and economic growth when their human and labour rights are safeguarded, allowing them to access decent work in safe conditions. Target 8.8 of the Sustainable Development Goals (SDGs) urges governments and employers to protect labour rights and ensure secure working environments for all, including migrant workers and those in precarious employment (United Nations, 2024).

INTRODUCTION

This story captures some of the complexities and issues of inequity and exploitation, informal work and the limits and possibilities of LLL in the region of Sub-Saharan Africa (SSA)—including at the foundational levels for so many young people who are forced into dangerous and precarious informal work at the expense of attending school.

In what follows we will engage with these issues and challenges in more detail, to identify the character and the contours of the informal economy, informal labour market and the challenges for informal workers to engage in meaningful LLL and skills development in SSA. In the following two sections we will reference the substantial academic and grey literature that suggests there are significant differences between regions and countries in SSA in terms of the percentage of workers who are "informal" (Kiaga & Leung, 2020, p. 11). In Southern Africa (40.2%) the share of informal employment is less than half than that in Central Africa (91.0%), Eastern Africa (91.6%) and Western Africa (92.4%). The share of informal employment reaches its highest rate in Burkina Faso (94.6%) and Benin (94.5%), while South Africa (34%) and Cabo Verde (46.5%) have the lowest rates. In both rural (88.3%) and urban areas (76.3%) informality is the dominant feature of African labour markets. Further, almost all of the agricultural sector in Africa is informal (97.9%) (ILO, 2020; Kiaga & Leung, 2020, p. 11).

At the same time, it is important to not fall into the trap of a primary focus on comparisons between African states—with their differing historical and contemporary challenges and opportunities—and/or to assume that there is a single, unitary "African story of postcolonial development" (Mkandawire, 2001). In doing the work of this chapter it is important, then, to acknowledge the problems of thinking about these challenges under the umbrella of a term such as Sub-Saharan Africa. The UN Development Program (2024) for example, refers to SSA as Africa excluding North Africa and including East Africa, Southern Africa, West Africa and Central Africa. This categorisation comprises 46 countries including: Angola, Benin, Botswana, Burkina Faso, Burundi, Cabo Verde, Cameroon, Central African Republic, Chad, Comoros, Democratic Republic of the Congo, Republic of the Congo, Côte d'Ivoire, Equatorial Guinea, Eritrea, Eswatini, Ethiopia, Gabon, The Gambia, Ghana, Guinea, Guinea-Bissau, Kenya, Lesotho, Liberia, Madagascar, Malawi, Mali, Mauritania, Mauritius, Mozambique, Namibia, Niger, Nigeria, Rwanda, São Tomé and Príncipe, Senegal, Seychelles, Sierra Leone, South Africa, South Sudan, Tanzania, Togo, Uganda, Zambia and Zimbabwe. The World Bank (2024), however, adds Sudan and Somalia to make a total 48 countries under this geographical classification.

In an article on *Quartz* that opens with an account of the ways that many commentators, academics, agencies and organisations, collapse the diversity of Africa under terms such as "Sub-Saharan Africa", Max de Haldevang (2016), citing Columbia University anthropologist Brian Larkin, argued that the term "Sub-Saharan Africa" was "confusing", "historically loaded" and racist. The term is often used in place of African country names by news media, and as a replacement term for "racially tinged phrases" such as "Tropical Africa" and "Black Africa" to denote a dividing line between a supposedly more culturally developed northern Africa. In seeking to explain demographic and economic trends the World Bank, ILO, UN and other international organisations have continued to reproduce this term to collect data, and to prioritise funding for development (de Haldevang, 2016; Tawiah et al., 2022).

With these concerns in mind, the provocation that we want to develop here suggests the need to identify and focus on the possible relations between TVET, decent work and just transitions and to explore what a new training, skills and political economy for an LLL agenda might look like in SSA. In that section we recognise the colonial history, and post-colonial legacies that continue to reproduce exploitation and inequality in SSA.

The Informal Sector and Skills Training in SSA

Given the number of workers in SSA who are in informal employment, and considering the challenges for inclusive and sustainable development in order to create decent work for all, the transition to formal employment remains an important focus in the policy space in Africa (Kiaga & Leung, 2020). The World Bank (Guven & Karlen, 2020) reports that informal work in SSA includes occupations such as truck drivers, market sellers, artisans and shop owners, weavers and tailors, fishers and divers, along with many others. Researchers argue that the rise of the Fourth Industrial Revolution (4IR) has contributed to job redundancies, skills disruption and jobs dislocation, so that many countries in SSA struggle with high unemployment (Debrah et al., 2018; Millington, 2017). The World Economic Forum (WEF, 2017) has argued that this high percentage of informal work is due to an inadequately skilled workforce, and an inability to capture human capital potential. The WEF's Human Capital Index measures the capacity of countries and economies to maximise their human capital through training and skill development deployed throughout one's lifetime (World Economic Forum, 2017). By this measure the WEF claims that SSA, on average only captures 55% of its full human capital potential, compared to the global average of 65%: "ranging from 67 to 63% in Mauritius, Ghana and South Africa to only 49 to 44% in Mali, Nigeria and Chad" (World Economic Forum, 2017, p. 1).

In an extensive review of the literature on the informal economy and informal employment in Pan Africa (including countries in the MENA region), Galdino et al. (2018, p. 232) observe that: "informal activities are viewed as a genuine way to make a living and establishing a business, especially in countries lacking governmental and institutional support", and that excessive "bureaucracy and corruption and inadequate legislation are all factors…driving people and businesses to informality" (see, also Kanbur, 2021). Galdino et al. (2018, pp. 235–240) identify a number of themes that speak to some of the challenges and opportunities shaping relationships between informal work and skills and training initiatives in SSA:

- *Institutional Environment:* Examine how institutional aspects such as public policies affect the development and growth (or decrease) of the informal economy.
- *Social Networks:* Networks of personal relationships that, through mechanisms such as trust, affect how firms and individuals engage in business activities.
- *Transition and the Informal-Formal Continuum:* Highlights the relationship between informal and formal economies and how they are part of a continuum.
- *Bottom of the Pyramid (BoP):* Most of the economic activity in the BoP happens in the informal economy, which is often the only option for individuals escaping poverty.
- *Gender Issues:* Gender discrimination and inequalities are important issues…The informal economy may bring women opportunities of personal and professional development.

The literature reports on diverse efforts in SSA to develop initiatives that seek to "formalise" the ways in which skills are developed and recognised in the informal sector, including recognising the testimonies of employers or master craftspeople (Alla-Mensah & McGrath, 2023). In Benin, for example, a collaboration between governments, businesses, NGOs and aid agencies and organisations such as the ILO has aspirations to "institutionalise" the "informal/traditional technical and vocational training sector" to "recognize skills gained in apprenticeships, which remains one of the most common and effective mechanisms for vocational training" (Palmer, 2020, p. 20). This partnership has resulted in the development of a system with two levels of qualifications:

1. a Professional Qualification Certificate (Certificat de Qualification Professionnelle (CQP)) for young people who have at least completed primary school. The CQP is a 3-year "dual-type" apprenticeship combining work experience with classroom training;
2. an Occupational Qualification Certificate (Certificat de Qualification aux Métiers (CQM)) for young people who have not finished primary school, have followed a traditional apprenticeship with a master craftsperson, and have had skills assessed. (Palmer, 2020, p. 20)

In another example, in Côte d'Ivoire, an initiative titled the Youth Employment and Skills Development Project (Projet Emploi Jeune et Développement des Compétences), seeks to recognise "informal apprenticeships via classroom training, formal certification, and a training wage for Apprentices" (Palmer, 2020, p. 21). However, there are significant challenges—financial, governance—that shape the success of these sorts of schemes. An evaluation of Ghana's National Apprenticeship Programme, for example, found that:

1. The difference in completion rates between those who received the subsidised training and those who did not suggest that apprenticeship fees present a barrier for many young people.
2. Trainer skills are a "constraint to the effectiveness of apprenticeships". (Palmer, 2020, pp. 21–23)

Martin Magidi and Innocent Mahiya's (2021) recent ethnographic study of informal workers/entrepreneurs and government, industry and NGO stakeholders in Zimbabwe provides a provocative account of the shifting and complex relationships between informal and formal sectors and workers—relationships that are largely characterised by a valuing and recognition of the formal sector/workers/training at the expense of informal sectors/workers/training. Their data—which is supported by studies elsewhere (Palmer, 2020, pp. 8–11)—provides evidence of the sorts of skills developed by informal workers in the informal economy, including vocational skills, soft skills and entrepreneurial skills (Magidi & Mahiya, 2021, pp. 509–510). Their work also provides evidence of the variety of ways in which skills are developed in the informal sector, including:

- Informal on-the-job training: involves one or more trainees working under a mentor who has expertise in the trade.

- Training workshops: the growth of the informal sector has seen formation of various associations that represent the actors in the sector which aim to improve the welfare of the sector, including by facilitating skills training among members.
- Self-training and learning through hobbies: many in the informal sector are self-trained, and have developed skills through a combination of strategies. (Magidi & Mahiya, 2021, pp. 516–518)

CREATING A MORE PROSPEROUS, INCLUSIVE AND SUSTAINABLE SSA?

This institutionalised and formalised framing and response to the challenges and opportunities of the informal economy, of informal work, and of the possibilities and limitations of LLL for sustainable development in SSA has produced, and continues to produce, processes in which international organisations have worked together in creating and implementing multiple programmes to create a more prosperous, inclusive and sustainable Africa. We review a number of these initiatives in what follows.

The African Union's *Agenda 2063: The Africa We Want*, and the 2030 Sustainable Development Goals share a common agenda of promoting inclusive and sustainable development and collective prosperity (African Union, 2024; African Union et al., 2023). The African Union, the United Nations Economic Commission for Africa (ECA), African Development Bank, African Development Fund and United Nations Development Program (UNDP) co-authored the *2023 Africa Sustainable Development Report* providing the first 10-year evaluation of the implementation plan of Agenda 2063 (African Union et al., 2023, p. vi). The report suggested "that progress on the Sustainable Development Goals and the aspirations, goals, and targets of Agenda 2063 has been uneven with significant differences among sub-regions and countries and among rural and urban areas". The report identifies that the challenges of multiple crises continue in Africa:

- the percentage of people living in extreme poverty is projected to rise until 2030;
- some 20 per cent of the population…is classified as food insecure;
- some 54 per cent of Africans lack basic sanitation services. (African Union et al., 2023, p. vi)

The report also found that "these challenges in recent years have [only] exacerbated wealth and gender inequalities and deepened rural–urban disparities in income" (African Union et al., 2023, p. vi). The *2023 Africa Sustainable Development Report* proposes numerous opportunities for improving African development prospects:

> Domestically, expanding the tax base, addressing debt vulnerabilities, deepening capital markets, curbing illicit financial flows and ensuring the full implementation of the Agreement Establishing the African Continental Free Trade Area can all drive progress, and investing in human capital, especially in science, technology and innovation, can help to unleash the potential of young people in Africa and build greener, more resilient economies. (African Union et al., 2023, p. vii)

The UNDP (2024), in the recent Africa green business and financing report, argued that the financial and market landscape and regulations are barriers to growing green business and that practical action will be required involving the themes of "governance, investment and finance, venture, corporate risk, enabling skills and market infrastructure". The UNDP (2024, pp. 15–17) states that each of the African countries, with the exception of Libya, has made a "commitment to climate goals and sustainable development and have a unique opportunity to utilize its human and natural capital, taking advantage of significant competitive advantages to become a global leader in the green economy". The UNDP (2024, p. 23) suggests that to "ensure that Africa does not remain dependent on imported renewable energy technologies and by extension become highly vulnerable to events such as supply chain disruptions", it will need to upscale, upskill and increase "funding for local manufacturing industries such that they have the necessary infrastructure, know-how and materials to manufacture these technologies".

In a recent Regional Economic Outlook report, the IMF (2023, pp. 1–5) argues that by harnessing SSA's wealth in critical minerals, the region "can supply the clean energy transition", and that the difficulty in making this transition is related to the lack of foreign direct investment to "upgrade" critical mineral "processing facilities" which can "spur technology transfer, job creation and skills development".

The African Union (2018, p. 8) argues that "the growing problem of youth unemployment is one of the main socio-economic development concerns of most African governments", and that the lack of "job-related skills" has restricted many young people and adults from benefiting "from the employment opportunities that offer a decent income". They further argue that "VET has to be sold as the magic instrument that converts youth into experts and entrepreneurs" (African Union, 2018, p. 39). The African Union (2018, p. 8) suggests that TVET reform is needed as the sector is "under-resourced", and "obsolete" with "damaged infrastructure" and "inadequate inter-sectoral linkage". In this context, there still remains a hierarchy in perceptions of parents, the public and some politicians, that academic qualifications are superior to vocational ones, and that "poor quality and efficiency of training has led to a situation where the labour market looks outside the country for skills" (African Union, 2018, p. 14).

The African Union (2018, p. 16) provides an assessment of past strategies including the Plan of Action for the Second Decade of Education (2006–2015). Here, the African Union recognised the significant role that TVET can play in supporting economic growth "as a means of empowering people to establish sustainable livelihoods". It claims that TVET should be "a high priority investment sector" during this decade, to address issues of equitable access, increased private sector involvement and funding, increased resources, integration in literacy and non-formal education and capacity building for teachers. In identifying a lack of success in relation to these challenges, the African Union (2018, p. 17) calls for a "new continental strategy" for TVET as a means "to facilitate the promotion of national development, social cohesion, political stability, poverty reduction and regional integration". The call for a "paradigm shift in TVET" would result in TVET preparing "young people to become job creators rather than job seekers", thereby putting "an end to the idea that, it is the under-performers and drop-outs of general education that will be found in TVET" (African Union, 2018, p. 20). Arias et al. (2019, p. 1) co-authored *The Skills Balancing Act in Sub-Saharan Africa: Investing in Skills for Productivity, Inclusivity and Adaptability* World Bank report which also argues that the issue of SSA's workforce being the least skilled in the world constrains the opportunity for a "growing working-age population… to reduce poverty and increase shared prosperity". Addressing this problem by building skills in SSA is possible, they suggest, "but it will require enacting system wide change".

Provocation: A New VET Agenda for SSA: Beyond Productivism and Extractivism?

Our intent to this point has been to engage with a number of the more apparent and significant issues and challenges that have shaped, and continue to shape, the character and contours of the informal economy, the informal labour market and the challenges for informal workers to engage in meaningful LLL and skills development in SSA. Issues and challenges that are made readily apparent in the historical and contemporary conditions in conflict/blood diamond mines that often involve appalling work environments, labour-intensive and dangerous tasks, meagre wages, managerial violence and a range of significant and adverse effects on local communities.

At the same time, we have alluded to a concern with how to include, and work with, the ways in which a colonial history, and postcolonial legacies, continue to reproduce exploitation and inequality on the margins of global capitalism in much of SSA. As we acknowledge these histories and legacies, a detailed examination of these *postcolonial development challenges* is beyond the scope of what we want to do in this chapter (see Alexopoulou & Juif, 2023; Ekuma, 2019; Fechner, 2022; Kapoor, 2008 for an extensive literature on a postcolonial theories of development that can inform future work). Our focus here is more limited, and is concerned with engaging work that references various elements of these histories and legacies as it seeks to explore what a new training, skills and LLL agenda might look like in SSA—if, for example, this agenda was to acknowledge how institutionalised skills development processes, practices and policies play not insignificant roles in what Simon McGrath and Jo-Anna Russon (2023) identify as the productivism and extractivism that characterise the Capitalocene and colonialism.

In this provocation we will introduce some of the key ideas and concepts that are suggestive of a framework for a new VET agenda for SSA (we will revisit some of this work in our final chapter). In addition, we will consider how some aspects of this work have been taken up and developed to explore the ways in which "thinking beyond the formal" dimensions of VET systems might provide productive pathways towards "sustainable Vocational Education and Training" (McGrath & Russon, 2023).

Simon McGrath and colleagues (2020)—drawing on an extensive research track record in relation to SSA, TVET, development, the Millennium Development Goals (MDGs) and the SDGs—present a review of the literature on TVET in Africa, and provide a productive approach that emerges from that review. At a fundamental level they highlight a concern in much of the research literature that in a context where "formal labour market employment and real wages have been stagnant (as in much of Africa over much of the post-independence period), it is perverse to see the provision of skills as the underlying problem" (McGrath et al., 2020, p. 469).

In SSA, the institutional (government, development agencies, NGOs) dominance of narrow "human capital" approaches to skills, individual motivations and a broader development agenda emerges from orthodoxies that seek to "explain individual rationales and economic dynamics in the most advanced economies without considering the extent to which these same forces operate in different cultures, education systems and economies". These models, they suggest, are "poorly suited" for the "challenges of increasing productivity and economic growth in African urban informal or rural subsistence settings" and of sustainable development (McGrath et al., 2020, p. 471).

They present a thematic analysis of mainly African-based research that can "support the improvement of just livelihoods in Africa", and which points to "ways in which VET can be theorised in relationship with economic, human and sustainable development, thus extending and expanding VET research in Africa" (McGrath et. al., 2020, p. 472). This approach/model offers much for shaping thinking about the relationships between the informal economy and workers, skills and training and ways of progressing the various agenda for sustainable development in Africa. They suggest that in order to build a transformative VET agenda, more needs to be done in breaking the dominance in development thinking of economics in order to productively engage "policymakers and practitioners", in the process of "economic transformation in Africa", and the relationships between Africa and the planet (McGrath et al., 2020, p. 481).

In building on this and other work, McGrath and Russon (2023, p. 1) have argued that VET in Africa "has been complicit in unsustainable practices due to its longstanding relationship with productivism, extractivism and colonialism", and in the ways in which since "the 1980s neoliberalism led to public VET adopting a skills for employability discourse". Their research, which we explore in more detail in what follows, provides case studies of regional areas in South Africa and Uganda, "with varying levels of formal and informal VET in both rural and urban contexts [with each generating] complex mixes of sustainability and employability concerns" (McGrath & Russon, 2023, p. 6).

McGrath and Russon's (2023, p. 3) work appears in a special issue of the *Southern African Journal of Environmental Education*, and they acknowledge that in TVET research and journals there is a marked lack of interest in examining TVET's possible relationships to concerns with sustainability. Given this evident lack of concern or interest in the relationship between TVET and the challenges and opportunities afforded by local, national and global sustainable development agenda, McGrath and Russon (2023, p. 4) situate the work that they want to do, and report on, in relation to a number of frameworks for identifying and exploring policies, practices and processes for sustainable education, including "the kind of sustainable education institutions" proposed by Stephen Sterling (2008, p. 65) which have the following elements:

- sustaining ("helps sustain people, communities and ecosystems");
- tenable ("ethically defensible, working with integrity, justice, respect and inclusiveness");
- healthy ("a viable system, embodying and nurturing healthy relationships and emergence at different system levels");
- durable ("works well enough in practice to be able to keep doing it").

In exploring these possible frameworks for the development and analysis of TVET's relationships to sustainable development, McGrath and Russon (2023, p. 4) also recognise what they call the "fragility" of "VET institutions across much of the globe, given VET's marginal location in both educational and economic fields". They argue that this marginality is particularly evident in Africa, and cite Stephanie Allais' (2022) identification of a number of factors for why this is the case, including:

- the slow pace and limited spread of industrialisation mean that there are few formal sector jobs, with majorities engaged in survivalist activities;
- formal VET has almost nowhere to send its graduates;

- the massive growth in secondary education has resulted in massified poor quality education. (McGrath & Russon, 2023, p. 4)

As they suggest:

> Not only are those entering formal VET less well prepared than they might be, but they are also coming in substantial numbers due to the breakdown in the formal school-to-work transition. Public VET institutions are expected to do the impossible, or at least delay the inevitable. Moreover, we also need to acknowledge that most vocational learning takes place outside the formal public college system. This is most apparent in highly informalised economies and learning systems. (McGrath & Russon, 2023, p. 4)

It is in this context that McGrath and Russon (2023) want to situate their description and discussion of what it is that we might take account of in thinking about a political economy of LLL in SSA. Foundational to this political economy of LLL is identifying what the concept of "skills for just transitions" might mean, might look like, in "complex labour market and vocational learning contexts" (McGrath & Russon, 2023, p. 4). Here, they cite the work of Mark Swilling (2020), and his suggestion that we should understand the concept of "just transitions" as:

> a process of increasingly radical incremental changes that accumulate over time in the actually emergent transformed world envisaged by the SDGs and sustainability. The outcome is a state of wellbeing founded on greater environmental sustainability and social justice (including the eradication of poverty). These changes arise from a vast multiplicity of struggles, each with their own context-specific temporal and spatial dimensions. (Swilling, 2020, p. 7)

In establishing this foundation, McGrath and Russon (2023, pp. 4–5) reference earlier work in which they suggest that taking up the challenges and opportunities that this idea provides for TVET, would mean "abandoning staples of conventional VET research such as school-to-work transitions, and skills for employability, productivity and growth". Instead, in developing a critical engagement with sustainability and just transitions, TVET research needs to "shift focus to questions of how vocational learning can promote decent work that contributes both to sustainable livelihoods for individuals and communities, and to wider efforts to restructure work and economic activities so that we live within our planetary boundaries" (McGrath, 2020, p. 8).

Having identified a basis for examining the promise and challenges of TVET contributing to "just transitions" in SSA, McGrath and Russon (2023, p. 6) identify, discuss and analyse four "very different cases of complex skills ecosystems in South Africa and Uganda, with varying levels of formal and informal VET in both rural and urban contexts". Their purpose here is to examine the ways in which each of these ecosystems "generate complex mixes of sustainability and employability concerns".

Gulu

Their first case is centred on Gulu, a city and district in the Acholiland region of Uganda. According to McGrath and Russon (2023, p. 6) the district is confronted by a range of significant conflict, development and environmental challenges. These challenges have produced "profound physical and mental health effects and concentrated land ownership in few hands". As a consequence, "unsustainable" farming practices, and limited access to domestic and international markets for produce, have resulted in the Ugandan government and some aid/donor agencies "encouraging large-scale agroindustry with little apparent concern for environmental issues".

In this context, the "formal VET system is characterised by small, poorly-resourced institutions" that are confronted by "longer-term" sustainability challenges, and which face difficulties in including an "environmental agenda" into the skills ecosystem. At the same time, a small number of initiatives led by staff, students and a limited number of national and international NGOs is attempting to introduce and develop practices, including in small agriculture contexts that are "more about sustainable livelihoods than decent jobs". In acknowledging the small scale and limited character of these developments, and the problems with embedding such change over the longer term, McGrath and Russon (2023, p. 7) suggest that these initiatives are, following the framework developed by Sterling (2008), "seeking to sustain people, communities and ecosystems", and appear to be "ethically defensible".

Hoima

Hoima city and district, in the Albertine Region of Western Uganda, is the location of McGrath and Russon's (2023, p. 8) second case, focused on the development of possibilities that are shaped by the extraction logics that accompany the location of large oil deposits in the region. In this context, "core tropes around employability are central, with environmental concerns effectively relegated to some window-dressing". Their discussion of this ecosystem centres on three development and skills projects funded and auspiced under the so-called British-German-Norwegian Skills for Oil and Gas (SOGA) programme. These projects, briefly, include:

- a programme for creating jobs through business development and skills training for micro and small enterprises, delivered by a Ugandan NGO;
- "staff at local VET providers and some students were trained to international standards in welding, electrical engineering and scaffolding. This training was offered by an international consultancy firm and a local Catholic vocational provider";
- "upgrading support was provided to the local public training provider in Hoima through an international NGO". (McGrath & Russon, 2023, p. 8)

In developing a more detailed discussion of these VET projects, McGrath and Russon (2023, p. 9) identify the continuation of an "extractive VET tradition", in which policy discourses are "very clear about the need to enhance employability or, rather, entrepreneurship, but there is little about environmental concerns". In addition, in the ecosystem they describe here, there is: "little sense of such issues"; "the broader context is disenabling"; and in "key local economic sectors such as catering, training has improved but livelihood opportunities largely have not". While an "eventual oil boom" might alter this ecosystem, "it would bring further problems and environmental challenges in its wake".

Durban

McGrath and Russon's (2023, p. 10) third case centres on Durban, the largest city and port in KwaZulu-Natal Province in South Africa. The city and province are shaped by a maritime history that is also characterised by "problematic settlement patterns, poor land management and ineffective regulation that has generated large areas of environmental distress, undermining the potential economic benefits of the maritime economy". In recent decades, including for the 2010 FIFA World Cup, Durban, and other parts of the province, has been the location of a "wider set of government infrastructural development plans through the National Development Plan…the National Infrastructure Plan…and the Oceans Phakisa initiative".

In discussing the details of several of these infrastructure initiatives, and the skills system policy agenda that has accompanied these plans and projects, McGrath and Russon (2023, p. 10) indicate that there is "robust evidence" of the emergence of a private-for-profit, and a state provided, formalised skills development ecosystem. They suggest, however, this is "an exclusive network, with limited engagement with both public skills providers and local environmental groups". Here, when "innovations for green skills training and green jobs do occur within private sector training academies, there can be a disincentive for collaborating with public providers where this may be seen as providing training for competitors". They cite research which claims that the "whole Oceans Phakisa model is one of extractivism with a very thin greenwashing" (McGrath & Russon, 2023, p. 11).

Alice

The Alice area of the apartheid era "homeland" of Ciskei in South Africa, is McGrath and Russon's (2023, p. 11) final case. The area, they suggest, "remains profoundly influenced by the legacy of the colonial Land Act of 1913", which "established such areas as labour reserves to exclude black Africans from urban residence while providing migrant labour for mining and manufacturing". Many of these apartheid "homelands" "were never economically viable as small-scale farming regions, remaining permanently dependent on transfer payments from migrant workers or, later, the state". Indeed, these "homelands" "were set aside for black African habitation precisely because they were not productive enough for commercial farming". These legacies have created significant economic, political and environmental challenges for livelihoods and "just transitions" for large sections of the populations in these areas.

McGrath and Russon (2023, pp. 11–13) identify that state agencies such as the Department of Rural Development and Land Reform, the

Department of Agriculture, Forestry and Fisheries (DAFF), the National Youth Development Agency and the Water Research Commission (WRC) are active players in an ecosystem in which opportunities are limited, and much of the "wider context is disenabling". Their focus in this case is on the different actors and activities enabled by the Imvotho Bubomi Learning Network (IBLN), that is "animated by Rhodes University and funded by the WRC". They indicate that a core feature of the IBLN model is the drive "for a closer relationship between formal and non-formal learning systems, in a way that resists hierarchical approaches prevalent in agricultural extension". In this sense, they suggest that IBLN is a "powerful example of a learning network" that "brings together these academic organisations with local economic development officers, extension services, farmers' associations, community radio and smallholder farmers around rainwater harvesting and conservation". The IBLN is, they suggest, an "environmentally strong" initiative that meets several of Sterling's criteria for "sustainable education institutions", as it "points towards more sustainable livelihoods and the potential emergence of innovative smallholder farmers into a third space within the agri-food system between subsistence and large-scale commercial production".

In discussing various themes that emerge from their studies of the diverse and complex ecosystems of Gulu, Hoima, Durban and Alice, McGrath and Russon (2023, p. 13) make a number of observations that are productive in thinking about the challenges and opportunities that characterise a political economy of LLL in SSA. Importantly, they suggest that their "ecosystems" approach to the analysis of "sustainable" TVET institutions and skills development programmes, and the ways in which these can contribute to "just transitions" indicates that the "wider political economy is also crucial":

> Where there are strong or emerging economic sectors, the building of greener providers may be possible. However, it is imperative to understand the nature of the global skills formation system for those sectors and ensure industry buy-in. Beyond that, though, lie even greater challenges of addressing inclusion and environmental sustainability.

In this sense, these cases suggest that "while the details of the dynamics of each skills ecosystem necessarily are unique", they can point to ways of thinking that are useful "well beyond the cases themselves in allowing new questions to be raised about regional skills systems globally" (McGrath

& Russon, 2023, p. 15). Possibly more importantly, and certainly more challengingly:

> what these cases show is the need to start prioritising VET, sustainability and just transitions, as the current academic literature is shamefully silent on this subject. If we are to break out of VET's complicity in the Capitalocene and extractivism, we need to start reframing how we think about VET and its purposes. (McGrath & Russon, 2023, p. 15)

REFERENCES

African Union. (2018). *Continental Education for Technical and Vocational Education and Training (TVET) to foster youth employment* (Addis Ababa: African Union, Issue). https://www.nepad.org/publication/continental-strategy-technical-and-vocational-education-and-training

African Union. (2024). *Agenda 2063: The Africa we want.* African Union. Retrieved 10 May from https://au.int/en/agenda2063/overview

African Union, ECA, African Development Bank, African Development Fund, & UNDP. (2023). *2023 Africa sustainable development report.* https://www.undp.org/africa/publications/2023-africa-sustainable-development-report

Alexopoulou, K., & Juif, D. (2023). Labour transformations in central and southern Africa from colonial to postcolonial times. In G. K. Bhambra, L. Mayblin, K. Medien, & M. Viveros-Vigoya (Eds.), *The Sage handbook of global sociology* (pp. 124–140). Sage.

Allais, S. (2022). Skills for industrialisation in sub-Saharan African countries: Why is systemic reform of technical and vocational systems so persistently unsuccessful? *Journal of Vocational Education & Training, 74*(3), 475–493. https://doi.org/10.1080/13636820.2020.1782455

Alla-Mensah, J., & McGrath, S. (2023). A capability approach to understanding the role of informal apprenticeship in the human development of informal apprentices. *Journal of Vocational Education & Training, 75*(4), 677–696. https://doi.org/10.1080/13636820.2021.1951332

Amnesty International. (2013). *Profits and loss: Mining and human rights In Katanga, Democratic Republic of the Congo.* Amnesty International. Retrieved 20 February from https://www.amnesty.org/en/wp-content/uploads/2021/06/afr620012013en.pdf

Arias, O., Evans, D. K., & Santos, I. (2019). *The skills balancing act in Sub-Saharan Africa: Investing in skills for productivity, inclusivity, and adaptability.* http://hdl.handle.net/10986/31723

Baker, A. (2024). Blood diamonds. *Time.* Retrieved 20 February from https://time.com/blood-diamonds/

Barrington, L. (2022, 21 February). *UAE becomes world's top trading hub for rough diamonds—DMCC CEO*. Reuters. Retrieved 20 February from https://www.reuters.com/business/uae-becomes-worlds-rough-diamond-trade-hub-dmcc-ceo-2022-02-21/

Benaicha, L. (2021, March 27). *Diamonds, best friend or mortal enemy?* History in Politics: A Durham University Society. Retrieved 20 February from https://historyinpolitics.org/2021/03/27/diamonds-best-friend-or-mortal-enemy/

de Haldevang, M. (2016, September 1). *Why do we still use the term "sub-Saharan Africa"?* Quartz. Retrieved 7 May from https://qz.com/africa/770350/why-do-we-still-say-subsaharan-africa

Debrah, Y. A., Oseghale, R. O., & Adams, K. (2018). Human capital, innovation and international competitiveness in Sub-Saharan Africa. In I. Adeleye & M. Esposito (Eds.), *Africa's competitiveness in the global economy* (pp. 219–248). Springer.

Ekuma, K. (2019). Postcolonialism and national HRD: Understanding contemporary challenges to skills development in sub-Saharan Africa. *Human Resource Development International*, 22(4), 321–342. https://doi.org/10.1080/13678868.2019.1612651

European Commission. (2024). *Migrant mineworkers advocating for decent work*. European Commission. Retrieved 20 February from https://international-partnerships.ec.europa.eu/news-and-events/stories/migrant-mineworkers-advocating-decent-work_en

Fechner, H. (2022). Legal segmentation and early colonialism in sub-Saharan Africa: Informality and the colonial exploitative legal employment standard. *International Labour Review*, 161(4), 615–634. https://doi.org/10.1111/ilr.12350

Galdino, K. M., Kiggundu, M. N., Jones, C. D., & Ro, S. (2018). The informal economy in pan-Africa: Review of the literature, themes, questions, and directions for management research. *Africa Journal of Management*, 4(3), 225–258. https://doi.org/10.1080/23322373.2018.1517542

Guven, M., & Karlen, R. (2020). *Supporting Africa's urban informal sector: Coordinated policies with social protection at the core*. https://blogs.worldbank.org/africacan/supporting-africas-urban-informal-sector-coordinated-policies-social-protection-core

ILO. (2020). *The impact of COVID-19 on the informal economy in Africa and the related policy responses*. https://www.ilo.org/africa/information-resources/publications/WCMS_741864/lang--en/index.htm

International Monetary Fund, IMF. (2023). *Debt dilemmas in sub-Saharan Africa: Some principles and trade-offs in debt restructuring*. https://www.imf.org/-/media/Files/Publications/REO/AFR/2024/April/English/MineralsNote.ashx

Kanbur, R. (2021). Introduction: The long discourse on informality as reflected in selected articles of the International Labour Review. *International Labour Review, 160*(1), 1–11. https://doi.org/10.1111/ilr.12227
Kapoor, I. (2008). *The postcolonial politics of development* (Vol. 1). Routledge.
Kiaga, A. K., & Leung, V. (2020). *The transition from the informal to the formal economy in Africa.* https://www.ilo.org/wcmsp5/groups/public/---ed_emp/documents/publication/wcms_792078.pdf
Kippenberg, J. (2018, May 10). Diamond trade still fuels human suffering. *Le Temps.* Retrieved 20 February from https://www.hrw.org/news/2018/05/10/diamond-trade-still-fuels-human-suffering
Laube-Alvarez, T. (2022, October 1). *The misattribution of Africa's natural resource wealth: An examination of the diamond industry.* Wilson Center. Retrieved 20 February from https://www.wilsoncenter.org/blog-post/examination-of-the-diamond-industry
Magidi, M., & Mahiya, I. T. (2021). Rethinking training: The role of the informal sector in skills acquisition and development in Zimbabwe. *Development Southern Africa, 38*(4), 509–523. https://doi.org/10.1080/0376835X.2020.1799759
McGrath, S. (2020). *Skilling for sustainable futures: To SDG 8 and Beyond.* TESF Background Paper Series. Bristol, TESF. https://doi.org/10.5281/zenodo.4022328
McGrath, S., Ramsarup, P., Zeelen, J., Wedekind, V., Allais, S., Lotz-Sisitka, H., Monk, D., Openjuru, G., & Russon, J.-A. (2020). Vocational education and training for African development: A literature review. *Journal of Vocational Education & Training, 72*(4), 465–487. https://doi.org/10.1080/13636820.2019.1679969
McGrath, S., & Russon, J.-A. (2023). TVET SI: Towards sustainable vocational education and training: Thinking beyond the formal. *Southern African Journal of Environmental Education, 38*(2), 1–18. https://doi.org/10.4314/sajee.v39i.03
Millington, K. A. (2017). *How changes in technology and automation will affect the labour market in Africa.* Institute of Development Studies. Retrieved from https://opendocs.ids.ac.uk/opendocs/bitstream/handle/20.500.12413/13054/K4D_HDR_Impact%20of%20automation%20on%20jobs%20in%20Africa.pdf?sequence=166%2526isAllowed=y
Mkandawire, T. (2001). Thinking about developmental states in Africa. *Cambridge Journal of Economics, 25*(3), 289–314. https://doi.org/10.1093/cje/25.3.289
Palmer, R. (2020). *Lifelong Learning in the Informal Economy: A literature review.* https://www.ilo.org/skills/areas/skills-policies-and-systems/WCMS_741169/lang--en/index.htm

Patel, N. (2018, November 21). *Figure of the week: Understanding poverty in Africa*. Brookings. Retrieved 20 February from https://www.brookings.edu/articles/figure-of-the-week-understanding-poverty-in-africa/

Sterling, S. (2008, Spring). Sustainable education—Towards a deep learning response to unsustainability. *Policy & Practice: A Development Education Review*, 6, 63–68. https://www.developmenteducationreview.com/issue/issue-6/sustainable-education-towards-deep-learning-response-unsustainability

Swilling, M. (2020). *The age of sustainability: Just transitions in a complex world*. Taylor & Francis. https://doi.org/10.4324/9780429057823

Tawiah, V., Oyewo, B. M., Doorgakunt, L. D. B., & Zakari, A. (2022). Colonisation and accounting development in Sub-Saharan Africa. *Cogent Business & Management*, 9(1), 2087465. https://doi.org/10.1080/23311975.2022.2087465

UN Development Program. (2024). *Africa green business and financing report*. United Nations. https://www.undp.org/africa/publications/africa-green-business-and-financing-report

United Nations. (2024). *8 promote sustained, inclusive and sustainable economic growth, full and productive employment and decent work for all*. United Nations. Retrieved 21 February from https://sdgs.un.org/goals/goal8#targets_and_indicators

United Nations Conference on Trade and Development. (2021, December 8). *Economic development in Africa Report 2021: Reaping the potential benefits of the African Continental Free Trade Area for inclusive growth*. UNCTAD. Retrieved 20 February from https://unctad.org/press-material/facts-and-figures-7#:~:text=Poverty%20levels%20declined%20in%20most,from%2083%25%20to%2080%25.

World Bank. (2024). *Sub-Saharan Africa*. World Bank. Retrieved 7 May from https://data.worldbank.org/country/ZG

World Economic Forum. (2017). *The global human capital report 2017: Preparing people for the future of work*. World Economic Forum. https://www.weforum.org/publications/the-global-human-capital-report-2017/

CHAPTER 5

Central and Eastern Europe (CEE)

Abstract The chapter begins with stories about Moldovan migrant workers to reveal not only their experiences of economic migration and informal and precarious work, but also the mix of social media responses to portrayals of their migration and circumstances—from sympathy and concern to anti-immigrant sentiment, even racism. This story captures some of the complexities of informal work, issues of exploitation and extraction and the limits as well as possibilities of a political economy of LLL in Central and Eastern Europe (CEE). The chapter reviews how the issues facing informal workers in CEE have been analysed by agencies like the ILO and OECD, and discusses policy pronouncements for developing "enabling environments" in which informal workers can engage in forms of LLL that promise to enhance their participation in more secure forms of work. Our provocation will suggest that the challenge in CEE is more than simply shifting people from informal to formal employment (the "formalisation agenda"). Rather, the challenge is to engage the full range of social partners in facilitating LLL arrangements that equip informal workers not only with accredited and certified skills, but also the capacities to participate in re-shaping new forms of decent work and social protection to escape "poverty trap" forms of informal labour.

Keywords Informal economy · Informal workers · Skills development · Political economy · Lifelong Learning · Central and Eastern Europe · Conscientisation

© The Author(s), under exclusive license to Springer Nature Switzerland AG 2024
S. Brown et al., *Informal Workers and a Political Economy of Lifelong Learning*, https://doi.org/10.1007/978-3-031-72451-0_5

89

Moldova: Shaping a Pathway to Decent Work in the Poorest CEE Country?

The ILO, in its most recent *Decent Work Country Program for the Republic of Moldova 2020–2024*, observes that "the development gap between Moldova and the rest of Europe has narrowed down", explaining that "in 2000, the country's per capita income was 14 per cent of the average EU income; in 2019 and 2020 the national income per person reached 29 per cent of the EU average" (ILO, 2021b, p. 5). However, the limited scope and scale of these developments have done little to significantly improve Moldova's overall situation. Demographic characteristics (the ageing of the population and ongoing high levels of emigration) together with "limited structural transformation (with a quarter of workers still employed in agriculture) combined with incomplete economic transition and governance reforms" continue to limit development opportunities (ILO, 2021b, p. 5).

Moldova provides a window on the challenges many people in the CEE region face in gaining access to decent work opportunities and conditions. Informal employment still accounts for slightly under 25% of the country's working population, with two-thirds of these being men. The ILO (2021b) identifies that the "large majority of informal workers (55 per cent) are own-account workers, followed by contributing family workers (13 per cent), of which women represent 75 per cent". The industry sectors most "exposed to informality are agriculture and construction with shares of informal employment above 60 per cent". For the ILO (2021b) these continuing high "levels of informality are also detrimental to the urgently needed productivity growth". Informality, in this context, "reduces incentives to invest in human capital, hampers business innovation and limits fiscal space for the public administration" (ILO, 2021b, p. 6).

Moldova's central economic challenge, according to the ILO (2021b), is low employment rates and associated economic inactivity. While the average employment rate across the European Union in 2019 was 53%, in Moldova it was only 40%, down from a rate of 45% in 2000. The picture is also skewed on gender and generational grounds. From the ILO's perspective: "Low employment rates are mostly due to the high incidence of youth, women, or older workers (55 to 64 years old) remaining out of the labour force. Close to 30 per cent of youth in Moldova are neither employed nor in education or training" (ILO, 2021b, p. 5).

Moldova can also be understood as reflecting the larger challenges facing the economies of the former Soviet republics. The economic difficulties of informal and temporary workers in post-Soviet economies such as Moldova were amplified by the COVID-19 pandemic, as lockdowns constrained the possibilities for work and commerce. The situation was worsened by the relatively weak nature of the country's job and income protection schemes. "Analysis of the impact of the pandemic on Moldovan labour markets shows that the loss in working hours quickly led to a reduction in employment. This is not surprising, as the country did not apply robust job protection schemes as other European countries did" (ILO, 2021b, p. 6).

A significant part of the story of post-Soviet Moldova is one in which large numbers of the population leave the country as economic migrants seeking to make some sort of livelihood elsewhere in Europe, or in other post-Soviet republics and Russia itself. This story of economic migration is a feature of informal work in informal economies in many of the regions of interest to us in this book. Indeed, in Chapter 6 we tell a story of women migrant workers in Southeast Asia, and the challenges, forms of exploitation and hopes that characterise the migrant experience. At this time, we want to approach this story of migration from a different perspective. A perspective that is important given that the tens of millions of migrants, refugees and displaced persons on the move around the planet are increasingly greeted with open hostility, anti-immigrant sentiments and racism, walls and barriers and periods of detention and attempts to expel them: *Go back to where you came from!*

As we indicated in our opening discussion of Bauman's (2004, p. 12) *Wasted Lives*, the experience of this anti-migrant backlash suggests that: "To be 'redundant' means to be supernumerary, unneeded, of no use...The others do not need you; they can do as well, and better, without you".

Journeyman Pictures (2016) describes itself as an independent film and video distributor of the "world's most provocative, incisive factual TV". At the time of writing its YouTube channel has more than 2.4 million subscribers. In June 2016 Journeyman Pictures (2016, n.p.) posted a video to its channel titled, *Moldova: The Devastating Effect of Economic Migration*. Its "abstract"/description of the video states:

> Tempted by opportunities in Russia and the EU, one in three Moldovans have left the country to seek work. As communities back home struggle to cope with the exodus, where does the future for Moldova lie?
> Raya is one of the 40,000 Moldovans supporting her family from France. "I've found cleaning work...that's how I earn my daily bread", she says. The money earned by those like Raya now accounts for 25% of Moldova's GDP—"without money from abroad", says Raya's mother, "we wouldn't

be able to survive". Yet communities have been left desolate by the exodus, and child trafficking is rife amongst youngsters with absent parents.

The film is an evocative, often emotional depiction of the experiences and consequences of economic migration and informal and precarious work. Since it was posted it has been viewed nearly 550,000 times, and there have been nearly 2000 comments posted in a number of threads.

It is this "unfiltered" public commentary that is of interest here. While many comments expressed sympathy, care, concern and despair for the lives depicted in the film, there was also a strong current of anti-immigrant sentiment, even racism, that itself provoked responses in support of, or against these sentiments. What these exchanges illustrate are the deeply personal responses to the ongoing mass movements of people around the globe, and the ways in which forms of racism, xenophobia and nationalism emerge and are used by various political forces—with little regard for the human lives, and the often desperate circumstances shaping these lives that are producing this mass movement.

@Jabzor, in a post from 6 years ago, said: *France needs moldovans Romanians and ukrainians not algerians*
That comment got 319 likes, and attracted 29 replies.

A selection of those replies is presented below. Given what we know about the increasing rise of racism, xenophobia and nationalism there is little here that might be surprising, but it does surface and capture the challenges faced by millions of economic migrants and informal workers.

@arbit3r
5 years ago
Very true.
37 likes

@ivanlagrossemoule
5 years ago
BlacknWhite Truthfully
Sometimes you have to be pragmatic rather than idealistic. Yeah, it's kind of racist, but what's the reality of France and the French in the end? Aren't they the only ones relevant in the issue?
25 likes

@dzimolai1184

5 years ago
Until the next World Cup or the euro's arrive, then you need the likes of Zidane, Mbappe, Henry.. Sacre bleu
4 likes

@BltchErica
5 years ago
@tx2128 It's much more different. Muslims are absolutely chaotic and force their religion once they migrate, trying to turn the place into their homeland. French people are also christian, so there wouldn't be much of a difference. Still, they shouldn't migrate to France. Moldovians could just migrate to Romania for example and live pretty decent lives while not harming the Romanian culture.
13 likes

@BltchErica
5 years ago
Also, Moldova is very small and has very few people in comparison to arabic places.

@mouloudaourtilane4394
5 years ago
they should have colonized them instead then. we algerians are paying for what the french did to algeria. and moldova chose it's path, be part of the soviet union, and leave the soviet union. we didn't have much choice. and you should see algerians differently, since algeria was france up until 1962.
11 likes

@mouloudaourtilane4394
5 years ago
Native British Identitarian we kicked them out because algerians were second degree citizen in their own country and had different rules to live by. before the french north africa was prosperous, and rich. the french ruined that, and you may not know it, but many (thousands) algerians died for france during WW2 against germany, because france promised it would in exchange give algerians the same rights as the french colons, instead when france won, it made a genocide "may 8th genocide" and they killed anyone who dared to speak up. now we have a shitty government and islamists are

gaining more power everyday. at the personal level, my grand pa was murdered by the french,he died under torture, and he wasn't even a soldier, it was enough for them to suspect you're a resistant to torture you until you reveal something or you die. and you should know that algeria never kicked the french colons out, most of them left because they were afraid, but the terms of the independance were clear about this part, the french colons had the right to live in algeria. actually i have a neighbor whose mother was a french colon who never left after independance because she felt like it was her home. i think the algerians in france should be able to remain there just like the colons are able to remain here.
5 likes

@MacakPodSIjemom
5 years ago
So, they colonized Algeria, and then left it alone. Algeria is independent more than a half a century, so as the French left Algeria, Algerians should leave France. Or to be kicked out of France, like the French were kicked out of Algeria.
1 like

@cernogoraz6980
5 years ago
why is it racist? these are our brothers, we are europeans from the same blood, same soil, same stories for thousands of years...why should we feel false brotherhood with arabs and africans instead? i would not expect or ask for the same from you, so why should i ask the same from myself?
3 likes

@cernogoraz6980
5 years ago
the difference is that the french left algeria and in 100 years it will be as if the french were never there...but in 100 years france will be an afro-maghreb mess
3 likes

@kathens7755
5 years ago (edited)

I find it funny how you unite all Europeans under this "white brotherhood", despite many Eastern Europeans being somewhat racially different with darker complexion and slightly different facial features, as goes for the Mediterraneans of the south. With plenty of northern Arabs or Turks actually having lighter skin and can easily pass for "white", or at least whiter than those aforementioned parts of Europe
Many of them aren't that racially different, and if a group of people can be integrated without degrading the overall secularism of a country I don't really care. This "but our blud and muh culture muh four fathers set" is all just feelings when you really get down to it
Just stop giving free handouts to everyone. If you actually set some standards maybe you might get some actual hard working people willing to fit in rather than the scrap leech scum of a country
There were a handful of places in the Arab world that used to be secular at some point, I wouldn't say all of their people are lost causes
5 likes

@anna-mariam4510
5 years ago
@tx2128 as a moldovan myself and living in Greece I can tell you that moldovan people are christian European people, yes. I have never encountered any problem with any European ethnicity because my ideas about God and life in general are pretty much the same. Maybe you are an atheist or even a Christian, it doesn't matter because all these centuries of christianity (orthodoxy is just the first original belief that started in byzantium and some countries obtained later) formed a specific mentality. The European mentality I would say which is very much connected to christianity even if you are not a christian. Moldovan people are poor and unlucky because of the complicated and difficult political situation in Moldova, but please if you want to say something about them, learn something right first.
1 like

@czthjvv
4 years ago
It's okay to be racist

Introduction

The Central and Eastern Europe (CEE) region is defined here in accordance with the focus of the ILO's Decent Work Technical Support Team and Country Office for Central and Eastern Europe, which serves 18 countries in Central and Eastern Europe from the Baltic States to Albania, and from the Czech Republic to Ukraine. The full list of countries includes Albania, Bosnia and Herzegovina, Bulgaria, Croatia, the Czech Republic, Estonia, Hungary, Kosovo, Latvia, Lithuania, the Republic of North Macedonia, Moldova, Montenegro, Poland, Romania, Serbia, Slovakia, Slovenia and Ukraine (ILO, 2023).

The informal economy in CEE is characterised by, among other things, seasonal migration, part-time employment, a high level of education of employees, trade union structures that are not adapted and do not have experience in how to work with the informal economy, and refugees (Glovackas, 2005, p. 4). A number of other characteristics of the region's informal economy are noteworthy:

- Many employees in the formal sector are paid part of their salary informally, meaning no tax is payable on it;
- Informal employment is particularly high in the agricultural sector: in the Republic of Moldova, for example, agriculture accounts for more than 60% of all informal employment;
- Similar numbers of women and men are working informally in most countries in the region;
- Women generally have lower-status jobs than men, despite having similar educational backgrounds. (GIZ, 2019, p. 44)

The COVID-19 pandemic profoundly affected the labour market in CEE. Women and lower-paid workers were disproportionately affected, and this exacerbated gender and income inequalities. Additionally, a number of CEE countries observed decreases in informal employment, and slight increases in the number of workers who were formally employed (ILO, 2021a, p. ix).

In this chapter we will develop a more detailed description, discussion and analysis of these characteristics, and their consequences, that primarily draws on the work done by agencies like the ILO and the OECD. In addition, we will discuss the sorts of policy pronouncements developed by these agencies and organisations as they seek to develop the "enabling environments" wherein informal workers can engage in the lifelong learning of skills that promise to enhance their participation in more formal, secure forms of work.

In this context, our provocation will suggest that the informal economy in CEE can be more usefully understood less as an undesirable form of labour and more as part of a repertoire of options available to people that they can and do call upon in parallel with, or as an alternative to, formal labour arrangements as their social and economic circumstances change. Equally, we will foreground the ways that some forms of informal labour can be, and are, associated with "poverty trap" arrangements that all too frequently are the only viable option for marginalised and vulnerable people across Europe, including refugees and migrant workers. These people face issues of racism and stigmatised identity, as well as long working hours and little if any social and income protection. In these circumstances informal workers in CEE experience significant challenges in accessing opportunities to acquire the skills they need to secure further training and entry into formal jobs with social and employment protection benefits. The challenge here is not simply to shift people from informal to formal employment (the "formalisation agenda"). Rather, the challenge is to engage the full range of social partners (including governments, unions, grassroots organisations and education providers) in facilitating lifelong learning arrangements that equip informal workers with accredited and certified skills, and the capacities to participate in re-shaping new forms of decent work and social protection that are inclusive of people who until now have been caught up in "poverty trap" forms of informal labour.

THE INFORMAL SECTOR AND SKILLS TRAINING IN CEE

Across CEE the post-Soviet era transition to a market economy has seen a growth in the number of private companies, but these have not been supported by regulatory frameworks and official monitoring of economic activity. Consequently, corruption, crime, political instability, a lack of trust in the justice system and rates of taxation and social security contributions have driven 'the rise and persistence of a high degree of informality in employment terms' (GIZ, 2019, p. 44).

The ILO has outlined the extent of the informal sector in the CEE in stark terms:

Although it is difficult to assess the extent of undeclared work in Central and Eastern Europe, recent findings indicate that informal employment is widespread in the Western Balkans and Moldova and also in other Central and Eastern European countries. For example, the latest ILO studies have revealed that over 30 per cent of the total workforce is employed informally in the construction sector of Albania and Bosnia and Herzegovina, as well as in the overall economy of Montenegro and Moldova. (ILO, 2016, n.p.)

An OECD (2021) report on informal work in CEE offers further observations regarding the social characteristics of informal labour, noting it is often enmeshed with traditions associated with the concept of *blat* which embraces kinship networks, tribal affiliations and the "favours economy" of the Soviet era (Glovackas, 2005; Ledeneva, 1998; Werner, 1998). Turning to informal labour was, in many ways, a cultural response to changed political and economic circumstances:

> After the collapse of the Soviet Union, lower disposable incomes, higher unemployment and the reduced purchasing power of official salaries and pensions gave rise to the (re)establishment of informal relations and networks to gain access to goods through particular groups providing privileges to their own kin. Moreover, networks were not only based on kin relations, but 'tribal affiliations, geographical proximity, shared schooling, shared workplace and friendships'. (OECD, 2021, p. 15)

The same OECD study notes how, following independence in the 1990s, post-Soviet republics "experienced a severe and protracted recession, high inflation and rampant unemployment. Given low rates of formal job creation, informality provided a certain safety net". Under these challenging circumstances, a "significant share of households turned to petty trading, which gave rise to informal commerce, and employment in the informal sector rose dramatically" (OECD, 2021, p. 15).

The COVID-19 pandemic severely damaged this safety net: "Previously, the informal sector has acted as a buffer in times of crisis and revealed its resilience in the transition to recovery, as it has offered subsistence revenues, flexible arrangements and opportunities for vulnerable workers and businesses alike" (OECD, 2021, p. 3). The pandemic produced complex consequences and challenges, including "pushing governments to close marketplaces and implement strict containment and social distancing measures" (OECD, 2021, p. 3). These impacted the informal sector especially (but often the formal sector as well). Informal workers were left with "no cushion on which to rely" (OECD, 2021, p. 3). At the same time, migrants in the "informal sector" had to "return home or remain in their countries of destination, both generating a loss of revenues in economies heavily reliant on large remittance flows". Alongside these concerns, "most government support programmes in the region focused on the formal sector, leaving informal firms and workers with little or no support" (OECD, 2021, p. 3).

The European Union (EU) emphasises that the educational challenges experienced by informal workers underline the importance of ensuring people complete at least their formal secondary education and have opportunities thereafter to engage in what the EU describes as either non-formal learning (i.e. planned activities focused on specific learning objectives and where some sort of learning support is available, such as workplace-based training programmes) or informal learning (i.e. learning arising from daily activities in work, family or leisure, but not organised as regards structure, objectives and learning support) (EU, 2012, p. 5).

In this context, the EU Recommendation on non-formal and informal learning (EU, 2012) encouraged member states to provide individuals with opportunities and arrangements for demonstrating learning obtained outside formal education and training (EU, 2012, p. 3). It envisaged governments developing arrangements for identification, documentation, assessment and certification of informal and non-formal learning to help people demonstrate their skills as the basis for engaging in further skills development and employment opportunities.

There is a social justice dimension to validation of non-formal and informal learning. The EU Recommendation noted, for instance, that "disadvantaged groups, including individuals who are unemployed and those at risk of unemployment, are particularly likely to benefit from the validation arrangements, since validation can increase their participation in lifelong learning and their access to the labour market" (EU, 2012, p. 3).

The most recent *European Guidelines for validating non-formal and informal learning* prepared by the OECD's European Centre for the Development of Vocational Training (Cedefop, 2023) underscores how validation facilitates lifelong and life-wide learning and employment careers that are more formal and secure. Beyond enabling efficient tailoring of skills development to each individual by avoiding unnecessary repetition of already established learning, validation is seen as helping people to understand their strengths and weaknesses, making it a helpful tool for personal development (Cedefop, 2023, p. 13).

For several development agencies, the needs and circumstances of informal workers in CEE indicate the requirement for a range of governmental and social partners to be involved in the design, delivery and evaluation of relevant skills development systems. In its *Toolkit*, GIZ (2019, p. 19) argues that skills development should involve a range of vocational education and training approaches:

- Formal vocational education and training provided by the state education system, leading to a recognised qualification. Learning processes in formal vocational education and training are goal-oriented and systematic;
- Non-formal vocational education and training outside the state initial education and training system. This is delivered by education and training providers, companies, social partnership organisations and public-benefit bodies. Learning processes in non-formal vocational education and training are also goal-oriented and systematic;
- Informal learning, i.e. non-structured, non-goal-oriented learning processes that take place at work or in other areas of everyday life;
- Traditional apprenticeships in which an apprentice acquires knowledge and skills in the workplace under the supervision of a master craftsman, master craftswoman or an experienced employee;
- Recognition of informally acquired skills tested and certified by an accredited institution based on defined criteria.

Examples of these approaches are not widely reported in literature on CEE. However, in Kosovo, GIZ (2019, p. 139) describes a project that aims to institutionalise informal education provision in training centres and vocational schools using a mobile delivery mechanism—the "Eco Trailer"—to deliver environmental education. Its aim is mainstream training courses in green technologies in Kosovo. The "eco-trailer" provides training on solar power, hydropower, wind power and mechanical energy and storage.

Capable of being used anywhere, the Eco Trailer's exhibits, experiments and models can be stored and assembled as required. Students can engage with training materials at various stations around the trailer. Its mobility allows it to be used at (vocational) schools, in teacher training and for PR work at events. Local teachers and professionals have received training in how to utilise the trailer's activities and to present the training materials accordingly. Every time the trailer is used it helps raise awareness about energy conservation. It offers examples of how renewable energy can be used and promotes options for fields in which private businesses could engage in the future.

The ILO (2021a) describes how active labour market programmes are being adjusted in CEE countries to provide for skills development to help people deal with the impact of COVID-19. In Montenegro, for example, informal workers have access to professional training through a universal and open internship programme. The ILO (2021a, p. 50) suggests that using labour market programmes in this manner helps to prevent the emergence of "a lockdown generation" by articulating responses to the needs of different groups of workers in the informal economy, including: "atypical non-standard/informal/seasonal workers; youth in transition from education to the labour market; long-term unemployed who do not receive unemployment benefits; persons with disabilities; families with one parent who is unemployed".

More recently, a report by the OECD, *Breaking the Vicious Circles of Informal Employment and Low-Paying Work* (OECD, 2024) provides new perspectives on informality and the importance of addressing skills imbalances. The report's Foreword makes several key claims, including: "First, it disassembles the mechanics of the deleterious links between informal employment, low-paying work and low skills. It shows that informal employment is highly persistent, and that the vulnerability of informal workers is passed on to their children in the absence of adequate education, skills and social protection policy". Second, the report "underscores the double burden of informality and low-paying work that a large share of workers in developing and emerging economies carry, and as such calls for policy solutions that go beyond the formalisation agenda and embrace the goal of social justice" (OECD, 2024, p. 3).

The fourth chapter of the same report examines the skills challenges facing informal workers compared with formal workers. It reveals that informal workers not only have "substantially lower levels of schooling compared with formal workers"; they also have fewer opportunities to upgrade their skills "whether through employer-provided training, public training programmes or other forms of learning" (OECD, 2024, p. 83). To overcome these challenges, and thereby redress the skills gaps that economies with significant informal sectors face, the report suggests that countries should take action on several fronts:

- continue raising the general level (in terms of quality and quantity) of schooling in order to strengthen foundational skills as a basis for future learning for all workers;
- encourage employer-provided training for formal and informal workers;
- make public programmes more inclusive for informal workers and their needs;
- recognise prior learning of informal workers;
- anticipate change in skills demand, and prepare the workforce accordingly;
- strengthen opportunities for more creative learning. (OECD, 2024, p. 101)

These kinds of policy approaches gesture towards social justice imperatives concerning informal work and lifelong learning. They also signal the importance of equipping workers with sound educational foundations (in literacy and numeracy) and the transversal skills required to capture new job opportunities (OECD, 2024, pp. 102–105).

Creating Enabling Environments for Informal Workers' Lifelong Learning

One of the more productive policy suggestions made by the OECD (2024) is for social partners and governments to collaborate in strengthening opportunities for "more creative learning" over the life course of disadvantaged workers. This approach, as we will discuss in more detail in our provocation, and our final chapter, underlines the importance of community-based lifelong learning approaches to facilitating skills development for informal workers. The OECD's report *Breaking the Vicious Circles of Informal Employment and Low-Paying Work* (2024) argues:

> For governments, it is necessary to create enabling environments for dynamic, active learning over the life cycle (ILO, 2018[50]). Together with social partners and wider community engagement they can help to reach out to more disadvantaged groups, such as informal workers, through dedicated lifelong learning centres (a practice that has proved successful in Iceland), comprehensive one-stop shops for guidance on lifelong learning (as in Portugal), family skills training programmes, community-based

approaches (as in Argentina (OECD, 2019[11])), and municipal digital hubs and libraries that enable access to digital technologies in areas with poor connectivity. Providing a legislative framework for paid educational and training leave, as well as financial support for various forms of training, is equally important. These efforts should be complemented by measures that would increase the take-up rate of "second chances" programmes, including among those who missed out on opportunities during the COVID-19 pandemic. (p. 106)

This report further argues (2024, p. 103) that a key challenge is to create opportunities within publicly funded skills training systems which mainly target formal workers "(even if only implicitly) by requiring people to have prior formal experience or credentials". Furthermore, informal workers are seen as less likely to take up skills training programmes because they "cannot forego a day's income, and cannot afford the costs of training and foregone income" (OECD, 2024, p. 103). For these reasons, among others, the OECD calls for "more inclusive training and skills programs", and suggests these can be "best realised through training funds and vouchers specifically targeted at informal workers with specific needs, and which can be accessible through non-governmental organisations (NGOs), co-operatives or various associations, including informal workers' associations" (OECD, 2024, p. 104). The OECD also sees opportunities for informal workers associations to help implement recognition of prior learning (RPL) by informal workers, noting that much of their skills formation occurs in informal workplaces. It suggests that "governments can either directly finance the related costs, such as assessment fees and certificates, or they can provide funds to other actors" (OECD, 2024, p. 105).

The situation of informal workers in the CEE region has been the subject of considerable academic and policy interest across Europe, with a strong focus on reforming the informal sector and facilitating transitions to "formalisation" of labour markets. For instance, in shaping an informal economy reform agenda for CEE, the EU's "cooperation programmes recommend not repressive and punitive measures but active measures to promote formalisation of companies and jobs through support measures, incentives and education" (GIZ, 2019, p. 44).

These approaches usually involve calls for significant public investments in education and training in vocational schools and local city-based training centres as well as vocational education in workplaces and training institutions. In parallel, according to organisations like the ILO and the OECD, it is necessary to develop more integrated and inclusive social protection arrangements that protect workers in the informal economy during crises such as COVID-19 so they can maintain incomes and enjoy the protection of their rights to decent work and lifelong learning (ILO, 2019, 2021a, p. xi; OECD, 2020).

Where informal workers have access to digital devices, they can access informal education and training via such platforms. However, because of issues related to digital literacy and inequitable access to internet connectivity for many informal workers, CEE states will need to prioritise enhancing digital infrastructure and assisting low-income informal economy workers (through business grants, for example) to purchase affordable smartphones so they can utilise digital platforms for skills development and economic activities.

Furthermore, ICT-based education approaches will need to be balanced with continuing support for vocational education in schools, TVET institutions and work-based skills development arrangements including: formal and informal apprenticeships; RPL processes; and active labour market programmes. Estonia, for example, has implemented policies to cover parts of the training costs for people already in employment. The government, in cooperation with Estonian IT companies, has launched an adult education project titled Choose IT. An OECD Survey of Estonia notes:

> Cooperation and dialogue between the government and employers and labour unions is likely part of the reason why this scheme has already had some success. The government and manufacturing industry has also recently launched a digital skills training project called DigiABC for unskilled workers, targeting the workers through their workplaces. These programmes may serve as inspiration on how to involve businesses more in adult education and training in cooperation with employers and labour unions. (OECD, 2019)

Given the buffer role that the informal economy can play in keeping informal workers in paid employment, the focus need not necessarily be on enabling informal workers to transition to the formal economy. Technical and Vocational Education and Training (TVET) is one option for enhancing the skills of informal workers with changing industry needs.

UNESCO has argued this way in shaping its recommendations on social dialogue, private sector and other stakeholders' involvement in TVET:

> Member States should, as appropriate, foster social partners' participation in TVET according to agreed labour market, education, training and other regulations.
> Increased private sector participation in TVET should be guided by key principles including alignment with public policies, support for social dialogue, responsibility, accountability and efficiency. When involving the private sector, TVET policies should recognize its diversity, including large, medium, small, micro and household enterprises engaged in all sectors of the economy.
> To enhance policy development and governance Member States should also, as appropriate, engage with other stakeholders, including non-governmental organizations, and representatives of learners, TVET providers, staff, parents, youth, traditional leaders, indigenous people and others. (UNESCO, 2016, p. 8)

Focusing on the full range of social partners—governments, donor agencies, trade unions and employer groups, among others—shows how UNESCO and other agencies imagine that training providers outside the formal TVET system can contribute towards co-designing and implementing approaches that support people in the informal economy to upgrade their skills and improve their working conditions. For example, soft forms of skills validation, such as skills passports, can be used to "make acquired skills visible to potential employers without requiring official recognition" (EU, 2018, p. 118). From the EU's perspective, in designing these sorts of skills development and recognition initiatives, it is important to recognise government-funded formal training systems are not the only or key partners in the TVET field. As one review observed, "because they are close to the intended beneficiaries, grassroots organisations, non-state organisations and the projects they manage are the most able to identify the needs—and especially the new needs—that formal training could satisfy" (EU, 2018, p. 119).

Provocation: A Political Economy of Lifelong Learning in the CEE Region

As our discussion vividly illustrates, recent accounts of informal labour in the CEE region have highlighted the ways in which informal work is entangled with the "substantial economic and social problems" associated with "the transition from socialist to post-socialist regimes" during which "many Central and Eastern Europe societies have developed a broad sector of informal work" (Pfau-Effinger, 2017, p. 387). For the sociologist Birgit Pfau-Effinger (2017, p. 388), these problems have been starkly revealed in Moldova "which has both a weak economy and a weak welfare state". She describes how "in informal employment, workers in rural areas, workers with a low level of education, young workers and older workers—in the final years of their careers and after the age of retirement—are over-represented". In this context, "It seems that a significant reason why these workers are often engaged in informal employment is the lack of alternatives in the labour market, particularly in rural areas, compounded by limited social benefits from unemployment benefits and pensions" (Pfau-Effinger, 2017, p. 387).

Accounts like these indicate the ways that informal employment and networks, within and across borders, are part of a repertoire of strategies available to people to meet their economic and social objectives, especially in the absence of adequate social protection. Pfau-Effinger's research reveals the different forms that informal work can take in the CEE region and the social, economic and political contexts in which these usually occur. Her theoretical approach "distinguishes different types of informal employment through their exposure to varying degrees of social risks, and different types and motivations of the workers and employers" (Pfau-Effinger, 2017, p. 389). Her typology describes the lower risk forms of informal work as "moonlighting" and "social solidarity":

> The 'moonlighting' type of informal employment is based on a second job which supplements a full-time job in regular employment...These workers have usually already paid social security contributions through their regular employment relationship, and are not interested in paying additional taxes and contributions. Their main motive is to provide a little extra income—for example, to afford a few luxuries—rather than to escape poverty. (Pfau-Effinger, 2017, p. 389)

The other low risk form of informal work "social solidarity"—involves "an exchange of services among acquaintances such as relatives, friends, colleagues or neighbours", such as when friends help each other to renovate their flat or house. Pfau-Effinger (2017, p. 389) observes that the principal motive here is "mutual support within social networks, rather than monetary gain".

By way of contrast, the "poverty escape" type of informal work represents the main source of income for large numbers of informal workers. Pfau-Effinger (2017, p. 389) highlights the structural dimensions of the risks involved in this form:

> The workforce engaged in this type of informal employment comprises people who are restricted from entering formal employment and who have an income below the poverty line (e.g. unemployed people on benefits or retired people with pensions below the poverty level). The main motive of this group is to escape poverty in a societal context in which they do not have acceptable alternatives in formal employment or on the basis of social security benefits. This type is mainly promoted by weak economies and weak welfare states.

Noting that this "poverty escape" type of informal employment has been "largely eradicated" in strong welfare states like Denmark, Pfau-Effinger (2017, p. 389) argues "in the context of less affluent CEE countries, the combination of a weak economy and a weak welfare state" has provided the circumstances that support the development of the "poverty escape" type of informal employment "and leads to the over-representation of workers with specific social characteristics in informal employment". One of the key social characteristics that Pfau-Effinger (2017, pp. 395–396) notes among these informal workers is their lower levels of education than workers in the formal sector (who usually have completed at least their formal secondary education). Even when informal workers obtain work in formal enterprises, it is usually in roles which require low levels of education.

Another social characteristic of informal work in the CEE that Pfau-Effinger touches on is how "migrants are over-represented in informal employment and that such work is more common in rural areas" in CEE (2017, p. 388). This brings us back to the increasing issues of racism, xenophobia and nationalism that affect informal workers, effectively keep them locked out of wage and social protection systems and limit their access to training and skills development opportunities in the countries where they work.

Pfau-Effinger's work, and the research she cites, suggests that, in countries like those in the CEE region, there is no single trajectory of economic "development" impelling people to shift from informal to formal employment. Rather, informal employment remains a part of the repertoire of survival strategies people can, and do, use when they need, depending on circumstances, to supplement their formal wages, or show solidarity with neighbours and friends, or avoid the poverty traps associated with weak economies and weak social welfare systems.

At the same time, as many agencies observe, people working in informal employment could benefit from having greater opportunities to accredit the skills they have developed informally, so that these could be recognised and valued in workplaces and training settings in ways which advance their opportunities to access decent work. The challenge and opportunity for CEE governments is to simultaneously strengthen social protection systems while also collaborating with social partners (including companies that employ formal and informal workers) to create and fund LLL programmes available through schools as well as through community-based adult learning arrangements. As the EU has argued, considerable economic and social justice benefits can flow from initiatives aimed at assisting people to assess, validate and certify the skills they have learned in workplaces and through life experiences, as a means for accessing further training and securing decent and safe work opportunities in the labour markets available to them.

To the extent that these sorts of arrangements are developed *with* informal workers and *by* informal workers, to enable students to reflect critically on their situation and develop skills for understanding and changing their economic and social situation, they could contribute to what the Brazilian educator Paolo Freire (1972) described as a "pedagogy of the oppressed". For Freire, who worked in adult education among poor and illiterate workers and peasants in Brazil, this approach was integral to developing a "liberating education" where teachers would work as partners with their adult students to co-create knowledge and understanding about the situations and structures that oppressed and constrained them. Through practices of dialogue about, and critical reflection on, their lived experiences, marginalised workers could come to critically understand their realities, and become conscious of the structures that limited their possibilities for participating in decent work as part of a rewarding life for themselves and their families. What flowed from this *conscientisation* was a commitment by the learners to making critical interventions into their reality to actively transform it so that it becomes more just (Freire, 1972, pp. 48–54).

Another aspect of the plight of informal workers that we have sought to highlight is the way that their access to LLL, decent work and just transitions are thwarted by xenophobic and racist responses to them in media and policy contexts. The implications of this for the health and well-being of migrants and displaced people have been brought into stark relief by the work of organisations such as Médecins Sans Frontières (MSF) which has reported on "a tragedy unfolding in Europe" (Abubakar et al., 2024, pp. 2465–2466). The Report:

> details findings from Médecins Sans Frontières medical humanitarian projects in 12 countries in Europe and Africa, as well as in the Central Mediterranean Sea. It takes stock of MSF operational experiences between August 2021 and September 2023, drawing upon routine medical and operational data from MSF projects, as well as accounts from MSF patients and medical teams during that period. The report highlights how, at every step of people's migration journey towards and within the EU, their health, wellbeing and dignity have systematically been undermined by the interlinking violent policies and practices embedded in EU and EU member state policies. (Benvenuti et al., 2024, p. 5)

Medical professionals writing in the *Lancet* about the findings of the MSF report rightly observe that future international agreements concerning migration flows should "require specific penalties and incentives to ensure countries and regional organisations such as the EU are held accountable by the UN". They also underline the role governments can play in addressing "the legitimate socioeconomic needs of the most economically disadvantaged citizens in wealthy countries and take charge of adverse and incorrect media narratives on migrants" (Abubakar et al., 2024, p. 2466). In doing so, these authors argue, EU governments should shift away from "a security-centric view", and instead address "the underlying economic, social, political, and environmental factors driving people to move, including conflicts, climate change, and development challenges" (Abubakar et al., 2024, p. 2466).

This is the sort of shift that a political economy of LLL approach engenders. It draws the attention of policy-makers to the lived experience of informal workers (often employed as migrant workers) being marginalised, oppressed, stigmatised and thereby excluded from access to education, training and support services that would enable them to develop the skills they need to secure decent work and lives. It locates their circumstances in the wider socio-ecological context of global capitalism. And it calls for responses which acknowledge and uphold our common humanity.

References

Abubakar, I., Langella, R., & Meda, N. (2024). Europe's anti-migration policies: The need to reverse a trajectory towards death, despair, and destitution. *The Lancet, 403*(10443), 2465–2467. https://doi.org/10.1016/S0140-6736(24)00922-X

Bauman, Z. (2004). *Wasted lives: Modernity and its outcasts*. Wiley.

Benvenuti, B., Marshall-Denton, C., & McCann, S. (2024). *Death, despair and destitution: The human costs of the EU's migration policies*. Doctors Without Borders (Médecins sans frontières). https://www.msf.org/death-despair-and-destitution-human-costs-eu-migration-policies

Cedefop. (2023). *European guidelines for validating non-formal and informal learning* (9289606029). Office for Official Publications of the European Union. https://www.cedefop.europa.eu/en/publications/4054

European Union. (2012). *Council recommendation of 20 December 2012 on the validation of non-formal and informal learning (2012/C 398/01)*. https://eur-lex.europa.eu/legal-content/EN/TXT/?uri=celex%3A32012H1222%2801%29

European Union. (2018). *Policies on the informal economy: A global review*. https://europa.eu/capacity4dev/file/88944/download?token=1Lb4yf8Y

Freire, P. (1972). *Pedagogy of the oppressed*. Penguin.

GIZ. (2019). *Toolkit: Learning and working in the informal economy*. https://www.giz.de/expertise/downloads/giz2019_Toolkit_Informal_Economy_EN.pdf

Glovackas, S. (2005). *The informal economy in Central and Eastern Europe*. https://www.wiego.org/sites/default/files/publications/files/Glovackas-Central-Eastern-Europe.pdf

ILO. (2016). *Informal economy in Central and Eastern Europe*. https://www.ilo.org/resource/informal-economy-central-and-eastern-europe

ILO. (2018). *Social protection for older persons: Policy trends and statistics 2017–19*. International Labour Organisation.

ILO. (2019). *Work for a brighter future: Global commission on the future of work*. International Labour Organisation. https://www.ilo.org/publications/work-brighter-future

ILO. (2021a). *Assessment of the social security responses to COVID-19: Lessons from the Western Balkans and Eastern Europe during the first stage of the pandemic.* https://www.ilo.org/wcmsp5/groups/public/---europe/---ro-geneva/---sro-budapest/documents/publication/wcms_775160.pdf

ILO. (2021b). *Decent work country programme for the Republic of Moldova 2021–2024.* https://www.ilo.org/resource/decent-work-country-programme-republic-moldova-2021-2024

ILO. (2023). *Central and Eastern Europe—Where we work.* https://www.ilo.org/budapest/countries-covered/lang--en/index.htm

Journeyman Pictures. (2016). *Moldova: The devastating effect of economic migration.* Journeyman Pictures. Retrieved 1 July from https://www.youtube.com/watch?v=SKzMShLaB6w

Ledeneva, A. V. (1998). *Russia's economy of favours: Blat, networking and informal exchange* (Vol. 102). Cambridge University Press.

OECD. (2019). *OECD employment outlook 2019: The future of work.* Organisation for Economic Co-operation Development. https://www.oecd-ilibrary.org/employment/oecd-employment-outlook-2019_9ee00155-en

OECD. (2020). *Informality and employment protection during and beyond COVID-19.* https://www.oecd.org/latin-america/events/lac-ministerial-on-social-inclusion/2020-OECD-LAC-Ministerial-Informality-and-employment-protection-during-and-beyond-COVID-19-background-note.pdf

OECD. (2021). *The sudden loss of a social buffer: COVID-19 and informality in Eurasia.* https://www.oecd.org/eurasia/COVID-19-informality-Eurasia.pdf

OECD. (2024). *Breaking the vicious circles of informal employment and low-paying work.* Organisation for Economic Co-operation Development. https://www.oecd.org/en/publications/breaking-the-vicious-circles-of-informal-employment-and-low-paying-work_f95c5a74-en.html

Pfau-Effinger, B. (2017). Informal employment in the poor European periphery. *International Journal of Sociology and Social Policy, 37*(7/8), 387–399. https://doi.org/10.1108/IJSSP-07-2016-0080

Werner, C. (1998). Household networks and the security of mutual indebtedness in rural Kazakstan. *Central Asian Survey, 17*(4), 597–612. https://doi.org/10.1080/02634939808401058

UNESCO. (2016). *Recommendation concerning technical and vocational education and training UNESCO.* https://unesdoc.unesco.org/ark:/48223/pf0000245068/PDF/245068eng.pdf.multi.page=5

CHAPTER 6

The Asia–Pacific Region

Abstract In this chapter, we begin with a story about the high percentage of migrant women in the informal sector in South Asia, their meagre incomes and lack of access to basic social protections. This story captures some of the complexities of informal work and a political economy of LLL in the Asia–Pacific region. For example, in the Pacific Island countries the formal sector is limited by job creation, underemployment and a growing number of disengaged young people. In East Asia and the Pacific, urban areas are experiencing population growth that is outpacing economic development creating significant challenges for low-income workers vulnerable to reduced wages and redundancy. We explain how international organisations are investing in LLL ecosystems and supporting people through the future of work transitions. We then discuss the limits and possibilities of the digitalisation of a political economy for LLL. In our provocation we argue that a political economy of LLL must acknowledge the limits and possibilities, the promise of LLL, and explore the complex intersections, the diversity of people in diverse contexts, their hopes, desires and aspirations for their futures.

Keywords Informal economy · Informal workers · Skills development · Political economy · Lifelong Learning · Asia–Pacific · Digital technologies

Women, Migration and the Informal Economy in South Asia
Since the mid-1990s, rapid industrialisation and urbanisation in Vietnam have led to a significant influx of migrant workers from rural to urban areas. The *We are Women* programme, funded by the UN Women's Fund for Gender Equality, and implemented by the Institute for the Development and Community Health, has delivered a range of benefits to around 10,000 female rural migrant workers in Vietnam since 2013. Benefits have included enabling these women to increase their access to social welfare benefits, legal protection, health care services and better job opportunities. The first community-based network for migrant women in Vietnam, established by the programme, now has 33 members facilitating regular group meetings to share information, advocate for migrant women's needs and build a supportive community (United Nations Women, 2024a).

The need for these sorts of programmes in countries such as Vietnam is evidenced by data which suggests that in South Asia, 95% of women are engaged in informal employment. Informal workers cover street vendors, small-scale traders, subsistence farmers, domestic workers and industrial outworkers. Women constitute a disproportionately high percentage of the informal sector workforce. In South Asia, over 80% of women in non-agricultural roles work informally (United Nations Women, 2024c).

In its account of the *We are Women* programme, United Nations Women (2024a, n.p.) introduces Hua, a 37-year-old migrant woman from Hai Duong province in northern Vietnam who moved to Hanoi with her daughter after her husband's death. Hua is described as living in a "shanty house in the An Xa neighbourhood with her 12-year-old daughter". Hua pedals around the city all day on her bike, selling brooms and boiled sweet potatoes, earning around six dollars on a good day. Another migrant woman, Hoa, explained that she moved to Hanoi over 15 years ago "because there was nothing to eat at home". Originally from a small village in Ha Nam province, 60 kilometres south of Hanoi, Hoa's small family rice paddy didn't produce enough to feed the family. In Hanoi she makes five dollars a day selling chicken and duck eggs, and with five other migrant women she rents a 25 square-metre shanty house in Phuc Tan Ward for $120 per month. Her husband and children are still in Ha Nam, and the remittances she sends to them means that the family is able "to make ends meet". Another migrant woman, Huong, who moved to Hanoi from Nam Dinh province seven years ago, claims that she "used to live among rats and garbage. As migrants, our jobs are unstable. As house maids, we can get cheated out of our salary or suffer sexual harassment in the hands of our employers".

Migrant women such as Hua, Hoa and Huong earn meagre incomes in the informal economy, and lack access to basic social protections. They are more likely to be self-employed (61.2%) compared to their male counterparts (33.2%) and many do not have labour contracts. With almost no social or work-related insurance, women face difficulties accessing healthcare services. The absence of traditional family support systems, coupled with low and unstable incomes, limited benefits and social exclusion, makes them susceptible to abuse and exploitation (United Nations Women, 2024a).

In Hanoi and Ho Chi Minh City, the two largest cities in Vietnam, an estimated 40–50% of migrants are women, facing particular challenges such as low and unstable incomes and a lack of social protection. As a result of participating in the *We are Women* programme, over 10,000 migrant workers in these cities have learned how to access social welfare benefits, legal protection and healthcare, to advocate for their rights and support each other (United Nations Women, 2024a).

For Hoa, being able to participate in the programme has meant that: "I have become more confident. I don't hesitate to share my ideas with others. I have also helped other migrant women with the knowledge I gained about our rights". In reflecting on where this increased confidence has come from, she emphasises the importance of group meetings, which not only provide new knowledge but also bring more joy, laughter and camaraderie into the lives of these women.

Shoko Ishikawa, the UN Women Country Representative in Vietnam, speaks positively about the outcomes achieved in and by the programme:

> We believe that our joint efforts will create a society where no migrant workers, and no female migrant workers in particular, are left behind. It is clear that there is much to be done to support this growing and vulnerable population, but with capable, skillful and confident women like Hoa, Hua, Huong and many others, a brighter future is within our reach. (United Nations Women, 2024a, n.p.)

The scale of the many challenges faced by women such as Hoa, Hua and Huong in the informal economies of South and Southeast Asia—at the intersections of complex historical and contemporary relationships and practices shaped by gender, patriarchy, social, cultural, economic, political and geographic forces—is, in a very abstract sense, made evident in the data about the informal sector and the numbers of women who seek to make some sort of livelihood through their precarious participation in these labour markets.

> UN Women is the United Nations agency "dedicated to gender equality and the empowerment of women". As a self-proclaimed "global champion for women and girls", UN Women was "established to accelerate progress on meeting their needs worldwide" (UN Women, 2024b, n.p.). According to UN Women (2024b, n.p.), there are "67 million domestic workers worldwide, of which 11.5 million are migrant domestic workers. Three out of four of these international migrants are women, and exploitation is widespread as many have no formal recourse or protection from the state". At another level, another scale, the details of these women's struggles, the stories that they tell, and which are gathered by various agencies, add further dimensions to what these challenges look and feel like. UN Women (2024b, n.p.) observes that, "many millions of women who set out across international borders in search of a better life. Lacking access to social services and legal protection, these migrant women are often subjected to abuses such as low wages and harsh working and living conditions. The worst abuses force women into sexual slavery".

INTRODUCTION

In 1942, the US and several European governments who were allies during World War II deliberated on how to rebuild education systems after the end of the war with the aim of achieving and maintaining world peace (UNESCO, 2021). By 1945 the United Nations (UN) Charter was signed and the United Nations Educational, Scientific and Cultural Organization (UNESCO) came into existence with the following countries in the Asia and Pacific region obtaining membership: Afghanistan (1948), Cambodia (1951), China (1946), India (1946), Indonesia (1950), Iran (Islamic Republic of) (1948), Iraq (1948), Japan (1951), Pakistan (1949), Sri Lanka (1949), Thailand (1949) and Viet Nam (1951). Other countries such as Bahrain, Bangladesh, Bhutan, Brunei Darussalam, Cyprus, Democratic People's Republic of Korea, Fiji, Jordan, Kazakhstan, Kiribati, Kuwait, Kyrgyzstan, Lao People's Democratic Republic, Lebanon, Malaysia, Maldives, Marshall Islands, Micronesia (Federated States of), Mongolia, Myanmar, Nauru, Nepal, Oman, Palau, Papua New Guinea, Philippines, Qatar, Republic of Korea, Samoa, Saudi Arabia, Singapore, Solomon Islands, Syrian Arab Republic, Tajikistan, Timor-Leste, Tonga, Turkiye, Turkmenistan, Tuvalu, United

Arab Emirates, Uzbekistan, Vanuatu and Yemen followed in the following decades, forming the Member States in the region (United Nations Department for General Assembly and Conference Management, 2024).

The informal sector accounts for 68.2% of the Asia–Pacific workforce with 1.3 billion people working informally. The region has the largest informal sector in the world, accounting for 65% of the global informal workforce (ILO, 2018b). The complexity and diversity of the Asia–Pacific region makes any generalisations difficult. Respect for these differences is important when discussing the challenges and opportunities for workers in the informal economy in the region.

The Pacific Island countries, for example, are characterised by a large informal economy with a formal sector limited by capacities for creating employment opportunities, underemployment, gender disparities in employment outcomes and a growing share of young people disengaged from or not in education, training or employment (Khatiwada, 2017). In Asian countries the informal economy is growing with an expanding workforce relocating to urban areas experiencing a boom in the service-sector (ILO, 2021b). The informal workforce has grown from "50% in the 2000s to 60% during 2010–2016" (Palmer, 2020, p. 3). Tremendous population growth in urban areas in Asia has outpaced the rate of economic development producing significant social challenges (ILO, 2021a). In East Asia and the Pacific these urban areas, particularly for low-income workers, are characterised by low levels of: economic inclusion (reliant on cash incomes and vulnerable to job losses and wage reductions); social inclusion (social protections, citizen participation and marginalisation for groups such as children, women, the elderly and rural migrants) and spatial inclusion (accessibility to housing and basic services and affordability, quality and safety of housing) (Baker & Gadgil, 2017, pp. vii–xxi).

Against this background, which is further developed in the following two sections, our Provocation in this chapter seeks to discuss the ways in which various international organisations and agencies imagine a political economy for LLL in the region. We build on our work with Pakistani colleagues on the (Broken) Promise of Education for Sustainable Development, to argue that the "promise" of a political economy for LLL needs to acknowledge what this "promise of LLL" might mean in different contexts, and for different people while identifying why this "promise" is often "broken", or remains limited and precarious.

The Informal Sector and Skills Training in the Asia–Pacific Region

The sheer size and complexity of the informal economy in the Asia–Pacific makes it difficult for education and training institutions to find the capacity and capability to provide skills training for the informal sector. A World Bank (2008) study, for example, raises concerns about the viability of restructuring education and training institutions to support skills training in both formal and informal sectors in terms of infrastructure, facilities, curricula, trained staff and resources. In these contexts, a common policy refrain is that TVET in the informal economy should be promoted, including through quality traditional apprenticeships in small, micro and household enterprises by engaging stakeholders in rural and urban areas (UNESCO, 2016).

Most informal sector workers acquire skills from the informal economy through family or community relationships, or their workplace, or informal apprenticeships, or through learning by doing (Bonnet et al., 2019; OECD & ILO, 2019; Walther, 2013). An informal apprenticeship is the main source of technical and vocational skills training in South and West Asia, but informal apprenticeships represent a small portion of informal skill development and training (Palmer, 2020). In China, Thailand and India, workers acquire skills informally on the job with as much as 80% of Indian workers obtaining skills informally (Gengaiah et al., 2018).

Palmer (2020) argues that informal apprenticeships should be upgraded to strengthen informal skills development for young people and adults in informal employment, alongside improving the capability of the formal education and training sector, and its accessibility to informal sector workers. Palmer (2020) references a number of innovative projects in South Asia that target traditional, informal apprentices to formally recognise and accredit out-of-school learning and upgrade skills in school-based training.

In Afghanistan from 2010 to 2020 a German-funded project, *Support to TVET in Afghanistan*, piloted a dual apprenticeships programme as a means to upgrade informal apprenticeship training. Traditional apprentices who have completed grade nine in formal schooling undertake a 3-year course combining classroom training for three mornings per week at a local vocational school. This programme offered a formally recognised pathway to further training and work (Palmer, 2020).

In Bangladesh the ILO, UNICEF, and the Bangladesh Rural Advancement Committee (BRAC) piloted the *TVET Reform Project* (2008–2015), a six-month dual apprenticeship training project as an approach to upgrade the standard informal apprenticeship. This consisted of two components:

- On-the-job training that included practical training delivered by a master craftsperson, and based on a structured format and training content using a competency skills log book.
- Off-the-job classroom training that included theoretical skills related to the participant's trade areas, in addition to life skills, financial literacy and basic English. (Palmer, 2020, p. 25)

The ILO's (2020, p. 56) Centenary Declaration provides a roadmap for COVID-19 recovery focusing on three areas of action to assist young people struggling to transition into employment: "(i) increasing investment in people's capabilities, (ii) increasing investment in the institutions of work and (iii) increasing investment in decent and sustainable work". Elements of action include investing in lifelong learning, ecosystems; supporting people through their future of work transitions—involving "a range of youth-targeted active labour market programmes"; tackling gender equality once and for all; and protecting the health and well-being (including financial resilience) of populations through social protection floors (ILO, 2020, p. 57).

The financing of skills training is a feature of debates about how best to move informal workers to more secure, or more highly skilled employment in the informal sector (ILO, 2018a, 2019b). These debates are often about equity, access, the cost for informal workers and organisations of undertaking/providing skills training, and the relative merits of demand- and/or supply-side funding approaches (GIZ, 2019). Citing an OECD (2019) report, Palmer (2020) observes that the challenges of financing Lifelong Learning (LLL) for 2 billion informal economy workers are beyond the capacities of most governments in low-to-middle-income countries (LMIC), and will likely require a mix of financing from governments, employers and workers, and the support of international agencies and governments. These are significant challenges, but there are some examples from the region of projects that work with this mix.

Since 2008 the Nepalese *Employment Fund*—the country's largest youth training programme, offering training opportunities to 15,000 young people annually—has conducted a competitive bidding system with various training agencies to provide skills development projects. The Fund—operated by Helvetas, a Swiss NGO, in partnership with the Government of Nepal, and financed by the United Kingdom's DFID, the Swiss Agency for Development and Cooperation and the World Bank—conducts a tendering process that calls for proposals, assesses proposals for viability and employment outcomes and evaluates proposals against criteria such as provider capacity and experience, labour market demand for the proposed trades, and cost (Palmer, 2020).

There are also several TVET reforms that address policy issues concerning the informal economy in Small Island Developing Countries (SIDCs) in the Pacific. A DFAT (2019) report considers a number of key policy issues concerning TVET reform in SIDCs including: understanding the vision and scope of the government's role in TVET; developing relationships between TVET and other education sectors; developing a national skills strategy; establishing a system of oversight bodies; ensuring that reform strategies are well resourced; and ensuring equitable access and inclusion. In this context, Samoa developed its "second Post School Education and Training (PSET) Strategic Plan 2016–2020"—aligned with the SDGs, "Strategy for the Development of Samoa 2016–2020", and the "Education Sector Plan 2013–2018"—to maximise PSET's contribution to achieving national development goals (DFAT, 2019, p. 8).

PSET had three domains (each with three goals and policy areas) "developed against the World Bank identified essential characteristics of an effective national workforce development system" (DFAT, 2019, p. 8):

- Strategic Framework domain (setting the strategic direction, prioritising a demand-led approach and strengthening critical coordination),
- System Oversight domain (ensuring efficiency and equity in funding, assuring relevant and reliable standards for quality, diversifying the pathways for skills acquisitions), and
- Service Delivery domain (enabling diversity and excellence, fostering relevance and enhancing evidence-based accountability for results).

Economic Growth, the Informal Sector and the Limits of the Digitalisation of Lifelong Learning in the Asia–Pacific Region

A significant feature of the literature on the informal economy, skills and training and the possibilities of sustainable development are debates about the intersections between the Fourth Industrial Revolution (4IR), the formal and informal economies, training opportunities and challenges for informal sector workers, the limits and possibilities of ICT-based projects and access to technologies and bandwidth (see GIZ, 2019).

Various features of those debates are important in understanding the relationship between technological progress and the informal sector, where technological progress does not necessarily result in a reduction in the size of the informal economy. For example, many workers remain in low-productivity jobs in a number of low-income economies because firms in the informal sector often have poor access to technology. Despite improvements in the business regulatory environment, little has changed to reduce the size of the informal sector (World Bank, 2019). The World Bank (2019, p. 26) argues that "informality persists on a vast scale in emerging economies—as high as 90 percent in some low- and middle-income countries—notwithstanding technological progress". India provides a good illustration of this paradox of a booming informal sector and continued poverty juxtaposed to technological advancement and surging economic growth. From 1999 onwards India's informal sector remained at almost 90% while experiencing many technological advances in its ICT sector, becoming a nuclear power, launching several satellites into space using a single rocket and breaking a world record in the process, and achieving an annual growth rate of 5.6% (World Bank, 2019).

Alongside this paradox there is a growing digital divide among Asian countries with Singapore, South Korea, Hong Kong, Taiwan and Japan making notable progress compared with other Asian countries, and between Asia and non-Asian countries (Maji & Laha, 2022; Nipo et al., 2014).

Given these existing and looming challenges, much of the intergovernmental policy literature continues to invest heavily in the promise of digitalisation in addressing, disruptively, the skills training challenges for workers in the informal economy. For example, The Deutsche Gesellschaft für Internationale Zusammenarbeit GmbH (GIZ) provides examples of three areas of digital transformation. First, informal enterprises can use apps to gather information on the availability and prices of goods, and use mobile phones and smart phones to communicate with customers, suppliers and other market actors. E-learning and mobile learning can enable informal workers to access general and vocational education. But poor digital literacy, lack of access to technology and connectivity and the purchase price of smartphones mean that many informal workers and micro entrepreneurs cannot reap these benefits of digitalisation (GIZ, 2019). Second, digital technology is crucial to the operation of the platform economy, providing many opportunities to informal workers. But while the platform economy opens up access to labour markets from which informal workers were previously excluded, it can result in more informal employment worldwide, thereby transferring insurance and occupational obligations to freelance workers (GIZ, 2019). Third, informal workers and informal firms have usually faced difficulty in accessing finance through formal banking systems. Digital innovations such as mobile payment apps are fostering the financial inclusion of actors in the informal economy, as it offers significant potential for marginalised sections of the population, particularly women and the rural population to make and receive payments for the goods and services they produce (GIZ, 2019).

A recent report by Global System for Mobile Communications Association (GSMA) revealed that while 96% of the Asia–Pacific population have access to a mobile broadband network, under half have yet to subscribe to a mobile internet service (GSMA, 2023). They list key barriers and policy actions to the uptake of subscriptions to close the digital divide as:

- "Knowledge and digital skills": with the introduction of nationwide roll outs of a Reliance Jio Digital Skills Program under the GSMA Connected Women Commitment initiative in India to assist rural women and marginalised or low-income groups of people to make use of digital access in meaningful ways;
- "Affordability of handsets and data: Kistpay, a financing platform in Pakistan, enables interest-free financing at scale for pay-as-you-go handsets, making smartphones more accessible";
- "Availability of local content": in Nepal, the Mamro Patro is a popular and comprehensive app used by the population to stay up-to-date with content and events;
- "Gender usage gap": women in South Asia are 41 per cent less likely than men to use the mobile internet. (GSMA, 2023, p. 47)

Research suggests that the range of limitations to introducing ICT in the informal economy in places such as Ahmedabad (India) includes: informal workers not owning smartphones or computers; many are not literate; and many live in remote areas with little internet access (Chen, 2016, p. 421). City-level policies and practices also "have a significant impact on informal workers" (Chen, 2016, p. 421). For example, a hostile "policy and regulatory environment serves to inhibit the livelihood strategies of informal workers…including their choice and use of technologies", particularly when items are seized by police (Chen, 2016, p. 421).

In this context Palmer (2020, p. 5) questions whether, in terms of what we identify as "the Indian paradox": "Will digital technologies actually change the informal economy? With such low use of basic technologies among the 2 billion in the informal economy, the answer seems to be: not yet". Indeed, "the hope that new technologies will soon change the face of the informal economy appears to be a little premature".

Elsewhere (Phillips, 2020) we produced a brief overview of the policy context and challenges associated with facilitating skills development, focusing mainly on the situation in relation to Small Island Developing Countries (SIDCs) in the Pacific. These include Cook Islands, Fiji, Federated States of Micronesia (FSM), Kiribati, Republic of the Marshall Islands (RMI), Nauru, Niue, Samoa, Solomon Islands, Palau, Papua New Guinea, Tonga, Tuvalu, Tokelau and Vanuatu. The international policy context for the development of TVET in this region was clearly articulated in UNESCO's *Pacific Strategy 2018–2022* which outlined commitments to advance Pacific Islands' TVET capacity as a key resource for facilitating sustainable development. As the Strategy states:

> UNESCO will…seek to support efforts to ensure that TVET provides quality education and training to match labour market demand, to better equip young people for employment both within their own countries, for overseas employment; and equip people with the skills for creating their own livelihood opportunities. Effectively reducing skills mismatch requires the creation of a comprehensive long-term strategy, one involving public/private partnerships among governments, employers, and education and training institutions. TVET is also important for ensuring social justice and sustainability. (UNESCO, 2018, p. 23; cited in Phillips, 2020)

While Pacific SIDCs are working to advance TVET provision in their countries on the basis of their national strategies as well as global frameworks such as the UNESCO Pacific Strategy, the SDGs and the UNESCO Strategy for TVET, the COVID-19 pandemic created significant challenges for the TVET sector globally during 2020 and beyond. In our review of the impact of the pandemic on the Pacific, we drew upon a joint ILO-UNESCO-WB Joint Survey on TVET and Skills Development during the time of COVID-19 (2020), which surveyed TVET providers, policy-makers and social partners, and received 1,349 responses from 126 countries in May 2020:

- About 90% of respondents reported complete closure of TVET centres in their countries as the pandemic spread. Partial closure was more commonly reported by respondents in some regions, mainly Asia and the Pacific, the Americas, Europe and Central Asia.
- There were disruptions to the provision of training, exacerbated by providers lacking the skills for remote training provision, having insufficient time to produce training videos, and having poor internet access.
- Respondents were concerned that demotivated students were more likely to drop out of TVET programmes.
- Low internet access among poor students was an impediment to remote learning.
- The closure of businesses during the pandemic made it difficult or impossible for students to complete workplace-based practical training—a critical element of TVET learning.
- Similarly, apprenticeship programmes were hampered by lockdown restrictions placed on enterprises. (ILO-UNESCO-WB, 2020, pp. 4–9; cited in Phillips, 2020)

In Small Island Developing Countries (SIDCs) in the Pacific, training was being provided partially remotely and partially face-to-face prior to the pandemic (ILO-UNESCO-WB, 2020, pp. 10–11). This mixed/hybrid approach gave Pacific countries more flexible options compared with those countries where there had been little take-up of distance learning prior to the pandemic (ILO-UNESCO-WB, 2020, pp. 10–11). Furthermore, some face-to-face provision continued to occur also in the Pacific. For example, in Kiribati, after an initial closure of educational institutions for two weeks, all training activities resumed as normal because there were no business closures. To facilitate COVID-safe learning experiences the Ministry of Health, WHO and Kiribati Family Association "provided information and training sessions to all staff and students about health and safety precautions related to COVID-19" (ILO-UNESCO-WB, 2020, p. 14; cited in Phillips, 2020).

Finally, this review of TVET in the Pacific region noted several critical considerations associated with enhancing TVET provision for developing skills matched to labour market, social justice and sustainability goals. The UNESCO *Pacific Strategy 2018–2022* (UNESCO, 2018, p. 16; cited in Phillips, 2020) sets out clear priorities for ensuring that TVET plays a crucial role in enabling Pacific Island countries to develop skills especially in their young people that are matched with the needs of labour markets and entrepreneurialism in their own countries and throughout the Pacific region. As well, TVET is recognised as contributing significantly to promoting social justice, empowerment and the capacity of people (especially young people) to participate in implementing policies that secure sustainability and improved quality of life in Pacific SIDCs. A key strategic goal in UNESCO's (2018, p. 44) vision for Pacific regionalism is to "support the transformation of TVET through the promotion of TVET policy reviews involving a broad range of stakeholders with consideration to increasing scope of modalities". Aligned with this are priorities to "support the use of ICT as an enabler of education", and to "promote regional and international recognition and accreditation of local TVET qualifications and facilitate knowledge sharing through enhanced regional and inter-agency cooperation".

A further priority is that "TVET sectors, through the appropriate national governance and management structures, are supported through the provision of policy advice, technical assistance and skills reinforcement to review and reposition the sector to provide relevant, quality seamless learning pathways and lifelong learning opportunities" (UNESCO, 2018, p. 57). These UNESCO priorities for TVET were reflected in the national development priorities statements of the Pacific Island countries, as detailed in the "Part V Country focus and alignment of development" section of the UNESCO *Pacific Strategy* (UNESCO, 2018, pp. 67–143).

Similar TVET priorities were also evident in the *Pacific Regional Education Framework (PacREF) 2018–2030: Moving Towards Education 2030*, which covers 17 Pacific island countries as well as Australia and New Zealand. Under the policy area of "learning pathways", for example, the PacREF prioritises developing "models for TVET that emphasize its value, relevance to industry and the labour market" (Pacific Islands Forum Secretariat, 2018, p. 9; cited in Phillips 2020). Similarly, it emphasises developing models for TVET which "facilitate opportunities provided by ICT" (Pacific Islands Forum Secretariat, 2018, p. 9), and it speaks of the importance of partnerships in the region with agencies like "the Australia Pacific Technical College (APTC), that have made and are making significant contributions to Pacific education and training outcomes" (Pacific Islands Forum Secretariat, 2018, p. 14).

And yet, even these sorts of investments and partnerships may not necessarily guarantee that TVET and lifelong learning will fulfil the skills development aspirations of young people in the Pacific, let alone those of informal workers (who were not the focus of our earlier review of TVET in the region). During the pandemic, in the Pacific region, "informal workers, as well as those with low work-from-home or high physical proximity service jobs" were negatively impacted (Arahan et al., 2020, p. 13). Similarly, jobs that were customer-facing were "particularly prone to disruption", as were jobs "often occupied by workers with lower levels of education". As women and young people were predominantly employed in informal work, the impact of the pandemic on them disproportionately "exacerbated existing inequalities in the world of work" (Arahan et al., 2020, p. 13).

While the learning opportunities that are being developed in the post COVID-19 Pacific context might offer informal workers the promise of pathways to decent work, the sorts of challenges and complexities touched upon here suggest that the promise might not always be realised.

Provocation: The "Broken Promise" of Lifelong Learning?

Our Provocation in this chapter seeks to build on our initial story, and our discussion of the ways in which various agencies and organisations think about the complex challenges, and often limited opportunities, that characterise the experience of the millions of informal workers in the Asia–Pacific region. An experience that is marked by significant diversity and difference, and which is shaped, fundamentally, by geography, but also by gender, ethnicity, religion, economic opportunities and political processes. As our story of the experiences, challenges and opportunities of migrant women in the informal economy indicated, their opportunities to engage in skill development and LLL are possible, but difficult. Can be limited, but also provide new ways of understanding learning and livelihood trajectories. In other words, a political economy of LLL should seek to acknowledge and identify what this "promise of LLL" might mean in different contexts, and for different individuals and different groups. And, at the same time, acknowledge and identify why this "promise" is often "broken", or remains limited, fragile and precarious.

In framing this Provocation we want to draw on our recent work with colleagues exploring the "broken promise" of education for sustainable development (ESD) in Pakistan (Anwar et al., 2023). In that book—*COVID-19 and the (Broken) Promise of Education for Sustainable Development: A Case Study from Post-Colonial Pakistan*—together with our Pakistani colleagues, we charted the emergence of the COVID-19 pandemic of 2020–2022, and the impact that it had on the lives of young people and their communities, education systems, the teaching profession and the responses by governments, NGOs and donor organisations in Pakistan. We situated this work in the development of Pakistan as a post-colonial nation-state in order to examine such things as education systems and policies, teacher education and notions of teacher professionalism, and to introduce a postcolonial critique of the UN SDGs as both a global and local framework for development.

The development of these purposes was framed by the telling of different stories at the beginning of each chapter—something that we have done here. Our aim was to provide a form, a space, in which our experiences, our memories, our recollections of family and personal biographies, the situated and entangled connections of our colleagues to the historical, cultural, social, economic and political life of Pakistan, could be written about in creative ways. Our intent there, as here, was to both open up the spaces for more scholarly work, and situate that scholarly work in the day-to-day challenges and opportunities that confront many of those who seek to promote, and to participate in, quality and inclusive education for all in postcolonial Pakistan, and in other postcolonial contexts.

Chapter 1 in that book was titled *Waadey*. This Urdu word translates as "promises". We used it to signal the various commitments and promises that are made by Pakistan's national and provincial governments to provide all young people with ready access to quality education, and to provide decent employment to young people through education and skill development. These "promises" are sometimes kept, but often broken. Especially for the most vulnerable and marginalised, and, in general, for young women.

As a means to situate our concerns with the often "broken promise" of education for many of Pakistan's young people, we told a "creative non-fiction" (Nelson, 2015) story of Feroz, a young adult male who was unemployed and appeared distressed because of his financial situation. Married with children, Feroz was dependent on his brothers and other family members for his livelihood because he had neither an income nor any financial support from the government. He had applied for multiple public sector jobs, even for very junior-level clerical and support positions but was unsuccessful because he did not have an effective *safarish* (political power to get benefit).

Feroz had completed his graduate degree in Pakistan but due to unemployment he migrated to Saudi Arabia, where he had worked as a semi-skilled construction worker for a number of years before returning to Pakistan for family reasons. After a gap of a few years, the Services and General Administration Department in the Civil Secretariat advertised over a hundred junior level (non-gazetted grade 1–14) positions in different categories. Feroz was among over three thousand young graduates seeking employment. He knew that without the *safarish* of a politician, or a high-level bureaucrat to help him, he had little chance of obtaining one of the positions. Desperate to find employment, he was introduced to the Minister's front man who was offering a job in return for a hefty *rishwat* (bribe). But Feroz did not have the money to pay.

We suggested that Feroz's predicament is symptomatic of how, in Pakistan, a significant number of graduates from elite public schools join the civil service, the military, medical and engineering professions, while others go to fields such as computer science or information technology. However, due to a very small number of openings in these institutions large numbers of young people cannot find employment in these professions. In Pakistan, the problem of unemployment for young people is increasing. Recently, a number of mass protests occurred urging governments to respond. In 2021–2022, for example, an ongoing series of protests took place in Gwadar (an important coastal city of Pakistan in Balochistan province), where young people were demanding their rights under slogans such as "Gwadar ko Haq Do" (give rights to Gwadar) and "Balochistan Ko Haq Do" (give rights to Balochistan). Of more than 20 demands of the protest movement, the most important concerned employment and livelihood opportunities for young people, the regulation of border trade with Iran, foreign fishing trawlers affecting the local fishing industry, and basic social services such as education, health services and water supply.

The protests emerged in the context of the multi-billion-dollar China Pakistan Economic Corridor (CPEC). CPEC is a flagship project of China's "belt and road initiative", and was signed in 2013 between the Pakistani and Chinese governments to connect China with the Arabian Sea via the Gwadar deep sea port. In return, China has committed to build Pakistan's infrastructure and support its socio-economic development. The port's establishment and CPEC have raised people's hopes with the promises for better employment opportunities in the informal and formal economic sectors.

In this situation, the protesters viewed CPEC as more of a curse than a promise of a game-changing socio-economic development strategy for the local population. These mass protests have produced fierce debate in Pakistan about how education and skills of young people need to be aligned with the required jobs in the port, and in other industries being established by Chinese companies under the CPEC. In Pakistan, educated young people do not consider technical and vocational education career pathways because there are only a few government departments that offer menial jobs that require certifications/qualifications from a designated technical institute. The private sector for these occupations does not require any formal certification or training from a designated institute for a young person to be employed. Anyone with experience can obtain employment and/or may be self-employed without any schooling. Many low-income families, particularly in urban areas, send their sons at a very young age to workshops—automobile, woodwork, plumbing, electrician and so forth—to learn skills and contribute to the family's livelihood.

In Pakistan the National Vocational & Technical Education Commission (NVTEC) provides policy direction and regulates and coordinates the Technical and Vocational Education and Training (TVET) sector. Pakistan has not prioritised TVET, or addressed the issues of quality education, or come to terms with shortages of institutions and teachers to produce a skilled workforce. Youth skills development is largely ignored in the formal Pakistan education system (Ministry of Education, 2009; NVTEC, 2009), and the TVET sector is incapable of developing youth skills in accordance with the national and international job market requirements (Ministry of Federal Education and Professional Training, MoFEPT, 2018). TVET is considered an educational and training system for young people who come from low-income backgrounds (National

Education Management Information System—Academy of Educational Planning and Management, NEMIS-AEPAM, 2021).

The National Skills Strategy (2009–2013) is the country's first policy document which aims to develop relevant skills to ensure the employability of skilled young people (NVTEC, 2009). However, skilling, reskilling and upskilling in Pakistan remain problematic because of gaps in the provision of relevant, quality training. The education system is ill-equipped to cope with technological shifts and labour market development (Ali, 2017; Bano et al., 2022; ILO, 2019a; MoFEPT, 2018). 80% of young people aged 15 years and over have low levels of education and skill training (Pakistan Bureau of Statistics, 2018), and youth skills development is ignored in the formal education system (Ministry of Education, 2009; NVTEC, 2009).

This brief recounting of Feroz's story, and a sketch of the social and cultural status of TVET in postcolonial Pakistan, provided a means to initiate a more detailed and extensive description and analysis of the intersection of a range of postcolonial legacies and patriarchal hierarchies that continue to produce and reproduce disparities and inequalities in certain locations and among specific population groups. In Pakistan, as in many other postcolonial contexts around the globe, these legacies include the political and bureaucratic governance system, social divisions between the elites and others, multiple divergent school systems for different socio-economic groups, and institutionalised, patriarchal forms of masculinity (Grewal, 2016; Sarangapani & Pappu, 2021). The gendered institutional structure favours male domination and produces and reproduces gender-specific educational institutions and professional pathways. In its civilising mission of "educating" the "natives", the colonial regimes in South Asia introduced European-based education systems, practices and processes and other projects of social reform. However, these had different outcomes for different classes, gender groups and ethnicities (Allender, 2021; Halai, 2012; Mehrotra, 2014; Topdar, 2015). The education system intersected with social reforms, and only allowed women from the upper class to participate in public spaces, while excluding the overwhelming majority of girls and women from participating in the process of schooling (Durrani & Halai, 2020; Khoja-Moolji, 2018; Saigol, 2016).

In postcolonial Pakistan, the global education policies of access, equity and quality of education are often in tension with national and local realities (Ali, 2017; Durrani & Halai, 2020). The neoliberal economic reforms in the 1990s aimed to produce skilled individuals to be productive in the market economy (Ball, 2012). These developments led to a shift in the location of public education policy beyond the nation-state, and created new partnerships in the domain of education and development to promote learning outcomes in education that were claimed to be in alignment with the "knowledge economy" (Verger et al., 2018). Consequently, transnational organisations and other new actors continue to influence the education policy context in different ways and produce a new regulatory role for the state (Olssen et al., 2012).

In Feroz's story, and in the stories of the women migrants that opened this chapter, there are indications of the limits of the dominant neoliberal account of skills development, and the concept of LLL as something that will readily be entered into by those provided with such opportunities. Elsewhere, in a genealogical critique of *the self as enterprise*—the subject of neoliberal governmentalities who is imagined as rational, choice-making, risk aware, responsible and prudent—we (Kelly, 2013) have discussed in greater detail the limits of these idealised, moral obligations to be and to become enterprising. In that critique we did not argue that the oftentimes powerful, and increasingly pervasive, incitements and exhortations to imagine the self as an enterprise were wrong. Rather, and in ways that echo much of our discussion to this point, and in ways that will be further developed in our final chapter, a political economy of LLL must identify the limits and possibilities of these neoliberal obligations to engage in LLL. And seek to identify and explore the complex intersections, in diverse contexts, of such things as gender, class, (dis)abilities, histories of learning and not learning, and the social, cultural and religious backgrounds that shape desires, hopes and aspirations, and the idiosyncratic and shared, orientations to particular education, learning and employment trajectories. We cannot assume that the "promise" of LLL—broken or otherwise—is something that is shared by all those for whom the promise is made (often on their behalf and without asking them).

References

Ali, S. (2017). The sphere of authority: Governing education policy in Pakistan amidst global pressures. *Globalisation, Societies and Education, 15*(2), 217–237. https://doi.org/10.1080/14767724.2015.1127575

Allender, T. (2021). North Indian educational liminalities: Western colonial experiments and a transitory dialogue with "The East." In P. M. Sarangapani & R. Pappu (Eds.), *Handbook of education systems in South Asia* (pp. 323–346). Springer.

Anwar, J., Khan, S. R., Shah, M. Z., Brown, S., Kelly, P., & Phillips, S. (2023). *COVID-19 and the (broken) promise of education for sustainable development: A case study from postcolonial Pakistan* (Vol. 7). Brill. https://brill.com/display/title/64453

Arahan, R., Doan, D., Dornan, M., Munoz, A., Parsons, K., & Yi, S. (2020). *Pacific Island countries in the era of COVID-19: Macroeconomic impacts and job prospects.* https://www.voced.edu.au/content/ngv%3A92829

Baker, J. L., & Gadgil, G. U. (2017). *East Asia and Pacific Cities: Expanding opportunities for the urban poor.* World Bank Publications. https://www.worldbank.org/en/region/eap/publication/east-asia-and-pacific-cities-expanding-opportunities-for-the-urban-poor#:~:text=Cities%20across%20East%20Asia%20and,Opportunities%20for%20the%20Urban%20Poor

Ball, S. J. (2012). *Global Education Inc.: New policy networks and the neoliberal imaginary.* Routledge.

Bano, N., Yang, S., & Alam, E. (2022). Emerging challenges in technical vocational education and training of Pakistan in the context of CPEC. *Economies, 10*(7), 153. https://doi.org/10.3390/economies10070153

Bonnet, F., Vanek, J., & Chen, M. (2019). *Women and men in the informal economy: A statistical brief.* International Labour Office. https://www.ilo.org/global/publications/books/WCMS_626831/lang--en/index.htm

Chen, M. A. (2016). Technology, informal workers and cities: Insights from Ahmedabad (India), Durban (South Africa) and Lima (Peru). *Environment and Urbanization, 28*(2), 405–422. https://doi.org/10.1177/0956247816566559

Department of Foreign Affairs and Trade, DFAT. (2019). *Technical and Vocational Education and Training—Practitioner level.* https://www.dfat.gov.au/sites/default/files/practitioner-technical-and-vocational-education-training.pdf

Durrani, N., & Halai, A. (2020). Gender equality, education, and development: Tensions between global, national, and local policy discourses in postcolonial contexts. In A. Wulff (Ed.), *Grading goal four: Tensions, threats, and opportunities in the Sustainable Development Goals on quality education* (pp. 65–95). Brill.

Gengaiah, U., Li, J., Hanvatananukul, S., Prontadavit, N., & Pilz, M. (2018). *Skill development in the informal sector in China, Thailand and India—A case study of street food vendors.* http://tvet-online.asia/issue/10/gengaiah-etal-tvet10/

GIZ. (2019). *Toolkit: Learning and working in the informal economy*. https://www.giz.de/expertise/downloads/giz2019_Toolkit_Informal_Economy_EN.pdf

Grewal, I. (2016). The masculinities of post-colonial governance: Bureaucratic memoirs of the Indian Civil Service. *Modern Asian Studies, 50*(2), 602–635. https://doi.org/10.1017/S0026749X13000772

GSMA. (2023). *The mobile economy: Asia-Pacific*. https://www.gsma.com/solutions-and-impact/connectivity-for-good/mobile-economy/asiapacific/

Halai, N. (2012). Schooling in postcolonial Pakistan and its struggle for identity. *NUML Journal of Critical Inquiry, 10*(2), 1–16.

ILO. (2018a). *Game changers: Women and the future of work in Asia and the Pacific*. International Labour Organisation. https://www.ilo.org/publications/game-changers-women-and-future-work-asia-and-pacific

ILO. (2018b). *More than 68 per cent of the employed population in Asia-Pacific are in the informal economy*. International Labour Organisation. Retrieved 22 September from https://www.ilo.org/asia/media-centre/news/WCMS_627585/lang--en/index.htm

ILO. (2019a). *State of skills: Pakistan*. https://www.voced.edu.au/content/ngv%3A87915

ILO. (2019b). *Work for a brighter future: Global commission on the future of work*. International Labour Organisation. https://www.ilo.org/publications/work-brighter-future

ILO. (2020). *Asia–Pacific employment and social outlook 2020: Navigating the crisis towards a human-centred future of work*. https://www.ilo.org/publications/asia-pacific-employment-and-social-outlook-2020-navigating-crisis-towards

ILO. (2021a). *Informal economy in Asia and the Pacific*. International Labour Organization. Retrieved 22 September from https://www.ilo.org/asia/areas/informal-economy/lang--en/index.htm

ILO. (2021b). *World social protection report 2020–22: Social protection at the crossroads—In pursuit of a better future*. https://www.ilo.org/global/publications/books/WCMS_817572/lang--en/index.htm

ILO, UNESCO, & World Bank. (2020). *ILO-UNESCO-WBG joint survey on technical and vocational education and training (TVET) and skills development during the time of COVID-19*. https://www.ilo.org/publications/asia-pacific-employment-and-social-outlook-2020-navigating-crisis-towards

Kelly, P. (2013). *The self as enterprise: Foucault and the spirit of 21st century capitalism*. Ashgate/Gower.

Khatiwada, S. (2017). *Improving labour outcomes in the Pacific: Policy challenges and priorities* (9221296733). https://www.voced.edu.au/content/ngv%3A77899

Khoja-Moolji, S. (2018). *Forging the ideal educated girl* (Vol. 1.0). University of California Press. https://doi.org/10.1525/luminos.52

Maji, S. K., & Laha, A. (2022). The role of digital skill in mitigating digital divide: Evidences from Asia-Pacific region. *Rajagiri Management Journal, 16*(3), 260–271. https://doi.org/10.1108/RAMJ-05-2021-0035

Mehrotra, S. (Ed.). (2014). *India's skills challenge: Reforming vocational education and training to harness the demographic dividend.* Oxford University Press.

Ministry of Education. (2009). *National education policy 2009.* http://itacec.org/document/2015/7/National_Education_Policy_2009.pdf

Ministry of Federal Education & Professional Training, MoFEPT. (2018). *National "skills for all" strategy: A roadmap for skill development in Pakistan.* Government of Pakistan. https://navttc.gov.pk/wp-content/uploads/2022/06/National-Skills-for-All-Strategy-2018.pdf

National Education Management Information System-Academy of Educational Planning and Management, NEMIS-AEPAM. (2021). *Pakistan education statistics 2017–18.* https://pie.gov.pk/SiteImage/Publication/PES%202017-18.pdf

National Vocational & Technical Education Commission, NVTEC. (2009). *The national skills strategy 2009–2013.* https://planipolis.iiep.unesco.org/2009/national-skills-strategy-2009-2013-5252

Nelson, M. (2015). *The Argonauts.* Graywolf Press.

Nipo, D. T., Bujang, I., & King, S. (2014). Global digital divide: Determinants of cross-country ICT development with special reference to Southeast Asia. *International Journal of Business and Economic Development, 2*(3), 83–95.

OECD. (2019). *OECD skills strategy 2019: Skills to shape a better future.* Organisation for Economic Co-operation Development. https://www.oecd.org/skills/oecd-skills-strategy-2019-9789264313835-en.htm#:~:text=The%20updated%202019%20OECD%20Skills,%2C%20population%20ageing%2C%20and%20migration.

OECD, & ILO. (2019). *Tackling vulnerability in the informal economy.* https://www.oecd.org/fr/publications/tackling-vulnerability-in-the-informal-economy-939b7bcd-en.htm

Olssen, M., Codd, J., & Anne-Marie, O. N. (2012). *Education policy: Globalization, citizenship & democracy.* Sage. https://doi.org/10.4135/9781446221501

Pacific Islands Forum Secretariat. (2018). *Pacific regional education framework (PacREF) 2018–2030: Moving towards education 2030.* https://forumsec.org/publications/pacific-regional-education-framework-pacref-2018-2030-moving-towards-education-2030

Pakistan Bureau of Statistics (2018). *Press release on provisional summary results of 6th population and housing census-2017.* http://www.statistics.gov.pk/assets/publications/population_Results.pdf

Palmer, R. (2020). *Lifelong learning in the informal economy: A literature review.* https://www.ilo.org/skills/areas/skills-policies-and-systems/WCMS_741169/lang--en/index.htm

Phillips, S. K. (2020). *Strengthening technical and vocational education and training (TVET) in Pacific small island developing countries (SIDCs) post COVID-19.* Retrieved 17 June from https://unevocrmit.wordpress.com/2020/12/02/strengthening-technical-and-vocational-education-and-training-tvet-in-pacific-small-island-developing-countries-sidcs-post-covid-19/

Saigol, R. (2016). *Feminism and the women's movement in Pakistan: Actors, debates and strategies.* https://www.fes-asia.org/news/feminism-and-the-women-movement-in-Pakistan

Sarangapani, P. M., & Pappu, R. (Eds.). (2021). *Handbook of education systems in South Asia.* Springer.

Topdar, S. (2015). Duties of a 'good citizen': Colonial secondary school textbook policies in late nineteenth-century India. *South Asian History and Culture, 6*(3), 417–439. https://doi.org/10.1080/19472498.2015.1030877

UNESCO. (2016). *Recommendation concerning technical and vocational education and training.* https://unesdoc.unesco.org/ark:/48223/pf0000245068/PDF/245068eng.pdf.multi.page=5

UNESCO. (2018). *Pacific Strategy 2018–2022.* https://unesdoc.unesco.org/ark:/48223/pf0000366463

UNESCO. (2021). *What is UNESCO? Our work in Asia-Pacific.* UNESCO. https://unesdoc.unesco.org/ark:/48223/pf0000260795

United Nations Department for General Assembly and Conference Management. (2024). *Regional groups of member states.* United Nations. Retrieved 30 April from https://www.un.org/dgacm/en/content/regional-groups

United Nations Women. (2024a). *Migrant women of Viet Nam claim social protection and rights.* United Nations. Retrieved 27 February from https://www.unwomen.org/en/news/stories/2016/8/migrant-women-of-viet-nam-claim-social-protection-and-rights

United Nations Women. (2024b). *UN Women Stories | The real-life tale of a migrant domestic worker.* United Nations. Retrieved 27 February from https://migrationnetwork.un.org/fr/hub/video?destination=/hub/resource%3Fresource_publisher%3D968&text=&gcm_objectives=All&cross_cutting_theme=All&region=All&country=All&other_language=All&embed_node=558&page=9

United Nations Women. (2024c). *Women in informal economy*. United Nations. Retrieved 27 February from https://www.unwomen.org/en/news/in-focus/csw61/women-in-informal-economy

Verger, A., Novelli, M., & Altinyelken, H. K. (Eds.). (2018). *Global education policy and international development: New agendas, issues and policies*. Bloomsbury.

Walther, R. (2013). Building skills in the informal sector. In K. Langer (Ed.), *Technical and vocational skills development in the informal sector* (Vol. 19, pp. 19–28). dvv International, Anton Markmiller.

World Bank. (2008). *Skill development in India: The vocational education and training system*. https://openknowledge.worldbank.org/handle/10986/17937

World Bank. (2019). *The changing nature of work*. World Bank. Retrieved 28 May from https://www.worldbank.org/en/publication/wdr2019

CHAPTER 7

A Political Economy of Lifelong Learning (LLL) for Decent Work and Just Transitions?

Abstract This chapter revisits a number of the aims and purposes of this book, and presents an overview of key dimensions of the challenges and opportunities that shape the informal economies, and the experiences of informal workers, of Latin America and the Caribbean (LAC), the Middle East and North Africa (MENA), Sub-Saharan Africa (SSA), Central and Eastern Europe (CEE) and the Asia–Pacific (AP). The chapter frames this discussion through an engagement with the ways in which skills, education and training and contested ideas about Lifelong Learning (LLL) are understood as being central to the problem of "informality", and as the "panacea" to this problem. We review our argument that conceiving of these challenges and opportunities as being structured by a "political economy" of LLL provides a productive avenue to draw on diverse, but critical, theoretical and methodological tools in developing our analysis. The chapter concludes by engaging with the work of McGrath et al. (J Vocat Educ Train 72:465–487, 2020), their identification of a number of emerging trends in VET scholarship in Africa—framed by a focus on *Policy, Systems and Institutions, Vocational Knowledge,* a *Critical Capabilities Approach, VET for Community Development* and *Skills for Sustainable Development*—and our exploration of how these possibilities might be productive in other postcolonial and development contexts.

Keywords Informal economy · Informal workers · Skills development · Political economy · Lifelong Learning · Policy · Systems and

© The Author(s), under exclusive license to Springer Nature Switzerland AG 2024
S. Brown et al., *Informal Workers and a Political Economy of Lifelong Learning*, https://doi.org/10.1007/978-3-031-72451-0_7

Institutions · Vocational Knowledge · Critical Capabilities Approach · VET for Community Development · Skills for Sustainable Development

Introduction

In 2020–2022 the COVID-19 pandemic pushed global, national and regional economies into a period of profound uncertainty and crisis that has since been compounded by high inflation rates, looming recessions, surging energy prices, labour shortages in different labour markets, supply chain issues, the Russian invasion of Ukraine, the Israel-Hamas War in Gaza and the unfolding consequences of the climate crisis. *The Lancet* (2022) has observed that a young person born in 2006 in Europe, "will have gone through the great recession...austerity...a pandemic with disrupted schooling and social isolation, a cost-of-living crisis, war in Europe, and a world coming to terms with the magnitude of climate change". People, young and old, around the world are growing up, living a life, amid an emerging assemblage of social, economic, political and climate crises—what the UN Secretary General has called a "code red for humanity" (Guterres, 2021), the European Policy Centre (2021) has identified as a state of "permacrisis", and the World Economic Forum (Torkington, 2023) calls a "polycrisis". Of course, the impacts, consequences and outcomes of this "code red" are differently felt and experienced by different age groups and different populations in different countries and regions.

As large parts of this book have illustrated, the pandemic produced an array of uncertainties, crises and disruptions, particularly to education, training and employment pathways (Allam et al., 2020). Furthermore, the massive inequalities and structural faultlines of the globalised capitalist economic model that the pandemic amplified, present significant challenges for the 2030 Agenda for Sustainable Development. An agenda that by many measures was under significant pressure prior to the pandemic (UNDESA, 2019). As we have demonstrated, many observers, agencies, researchers and commentators offer various proposals for meeting these challenges, and our engagement to this point has highlighted a number of them.

In Chapter 2 we identified the character and the contours of the informal economy, the informal labour market and the challenges for informal workers to engage in meaningful LLL and skills development in Latin America and the Caribbean (LAC). We opened the spaces for this discussion by telling a story of Haiti's contemporary social, cultural, economic and political situation, and the (im)possibilities for any real progress in relation to these significant environmental and political challenges. Our provocation argued that the litany of disaster, suffering, despair and an almost total lack of hope in what might be done, and by whom, to relieve despair on the scales evident in places such as Haiti appear not to be amenable to the sorts of remedies that organisations such as the World Bank propose. In examining the influence of the *Washington Consensus* in shaping the LAC's "lost decade" and the political economy of LLL in LAC, we proposed that the historical actions of many of these organisations have, indeed, produced these challenges.

Chapter 3 began with a story about Mohammed Bouazizi, a 26-year-old Tunisian street trader who, in December 2010, self-immolated in protest over his mistreatment and exploitation by local police and officials. Our intent was this story could open a window into an overview of the challenges and opportunities that characterise the Middle East and North Africa's (MENA) informal economy, informal work, the ways in which different populations experience these labour relations and practices and the opportunities that exist, or don't, for engaging in LLL as a means to develop skills that might lead to decent work and just transitions. In that chapter's provocation we indicated that the skills needs of informal workers in MENA should be understood in the context of the region's political economy, and the ways that LLL approaches can assist them to adapt to the changing structure and opportunities associated with the Fourth Industrial Revolution, as well as to recover from conflicts such as between Israel and Hamas in Gaza.

In Chapter 4, in telling a story about the political economy of blood diamonds, we set out to illustrate how a continent such as Africa, rich and abundant in natural resources, continues to struggle with forms of exploitation, a lack of transparency in global supply chains, often dangerous and largely unregulated labour practices, inequities and widespread poverty. This story captures some of the complexities of informal work, issues of exploitation and extraction and the limits, as well as possibilities, of a political economy of LLL in Sub-Saharan Africa (SSA). In doing this, we described some of the shifting and complex relationships between the informal and formal economy in SSA that recognises formal workers at the expense of informal workers. In our provocation we drew on critical analyses of VET in SSA to argue for a need to prioritise concepts such as decent work and just transitions, if we are to counter VET's complicity in the Capitalocene and extractivism.

Chapter 5 opened with stories about Moldovan migrant workers that revealed not only their experiences of economic migration and informal and precarious work, but also the mix of public responses to portrayals of their migration and circumstances—from sympathy and concern, to anti-immigrant sentiment, racism and xenophobia. This story captured some of the complexities of informal work, issues of exploitation and extraction and the challenges and opportunities of a political economy of LLL in Central and Eastern Europe (CEE). Our provocation suggested that the challenge in CEE is more than simply shifting people from informal to formal employment (the "formalisation agenda"). Rather, the challenge is to engage the full range of social partners in facilitating LLL arrangements that equip informal workers not only with accredited and certified skills, but also the capacities to participate in re-shaping new forms of decent work and just transitions to escape "poverty trap" forms of informal labour.

In Chapter 6 we constructed a story about the high percentage of migrant women in the informal sector in South Asia, their meagre incomes and lack of access to basic social protections. This story captured some of the complexities of informal work and a political economy for LLL in the Asia–Pacific region. For example, in the Pacific Island countries the formal sector is limited by job creation, underemployment and a growing number of disengaged young people. In East Asia and the Pacific, urban areas are experiencing population growth that is outpacing economic development creating significant challenges for low-income workers vulnerable to reduced wages and redundancy. In our provocation we argued that a political economy of LLL must acknowledge the challenges and opportunities of the "promise" of LLL, and explore the complex intersections, the diversity of people in diverse contexts, their hope, desires and aspirations for their futures.

Most often in Euro-American social scientific knowledge practices (Law, 2004), the idea of "story-telling" is displaced by the practice of "valid", evidence-based, reports and accounts that deny their story-telling attributes in favour of claims to truthfulness, validity, representativeness and generalisability. And while these can be appropriate genres and forms of knowledge production, they are not the only possibilities, and they might not be the most productive possibilities at all times, for all purposes. In telling the stories of informal workers, and getting inside the episodes that reveal their particular economic, social, cultural and ecological circumstances, we have sought to bring out the entangled aspects of their experiences of LLL, work and participation in everyday life. We have seen how people's involvement in informal work is inseparable from the challenges and opportunities they have faced in the places where they live. Adapting the methods and intention of E. P. Thompson's (1968) "history from below", we have sought to understand the diversity of experiences of informal workers in often precarious employment situations. In considering how people are engaged in informal work we also drew upon the work of sociologists such as Pfau-Effinger to understand the various forms that informal work can take—including "moonlighting", "solidarity" and "poverty trap" types of informal labour. And here, especially in relation to "poverty trap" employment arrangements, we identified the relevance of the work of radical adult literacy theorists such as Paulo Freire (1972), and their influences on thinking critically about a political economy of LLL. In a Freirian tradition, if workers in informal employment arrangements are to be enabled to develop the skills they require for decent work and just transitions, they need first to be engaged in developing diverse forms of consciousness of the structures that constrain and limit their opportunities.

Carlos Alberto Torres and Li Yan (2022), in a recent review of *Paulo Freire and the state-of-the-art of the international journal of lifelong education*, provide a productive account of a number of key themes that emerge from their analysis of the debates, critiques and uses of Freire's work in that journal over four decades. Our interests here are not solely with Freire, and/or his scholarship and its significant impact on adult education and LLL, and/or the character of the critiques of his work—including what some have identified as his silences on gender, and a uni-dimensional understanding of oppression that is informed by an often unacknowledged *Western episteme* that rests upon the "theoretical underpinnings of modernism and neo-Marxism" (Torres & Yan, 2022, p. 658). Indeed, the extensive and significant scholarship on Freire and LLL, including beyond the spaces of the *International Journal of Lifelong Education*, and the ways in which postmodernist, poststructuralist, feminist, postcolonial and decolonial pedagogies have encountered, engaged with and departed from Freirian critical pedagogy attests to the productive possibilities that can emerge from these sorts of critical encounters in adult education and LLL in different places, cultures, economies and ecosystems.

As we indicated in Chapter 1, our intentions here have been both more expansive than a narrow focus on pedagogies in LLL, and more modest in-so-far as we understand the contribution that we seek to make to ongoing debates about informal economies, informal workers and a political economy of LLL for decent work and just transitions. At the same time, we want to acknowledge that in our professional development, and in the commitments that we share to what the "promise" of LLL for decent work and just transitions can be, even if it often fails to deliver on that "promise", we have strong affinities with the "critical praxis" of LLL that Peter Mayo (1994, p. 139) identifies in his attempts to "synthesise" the radical pedagogical possibilities in adult education of the legacies of Antonio Gramsci and Freire:

> The first and obvious point that emerges from their writing is that adult education, as all education, for that matter, is not neutral and is very much tied to the hegemonic/ counter-hegemonic interests within a given society. A theory of radical adult education should be born out of a recognition of this point and should be inspired by theoretical perspectives that highlight the strong relationship that exists between knowledge, culture and power, rendering the kind of knowledge provided by mainstream institutions and the manner of its dissemination problematic. Radical adult education initiatives, therefore, underline a commitment to a cause. The common cause in Gramsci's and Freire's writings is the struggle against oppression caused by the exploitation of 'subaltern' groups by dominant, hegemonic ones. Radical adult education initiatives, developed on Gramscian-Freirean lines, should therefore be sustained by a theory which is imbued with a 'language of possibility' and emphasizes a strong commitment to the emancipation of subaltern groups from hegemonic domination.

In drawing this book to a close we want to finish with one way of conceiving a "language of possibility" for the ongoing, ceaseless, work of articulating and delivering on the promise of LLL for decent work and just transitions.

SKILLS AND TRAINING FOR DECENT
WORK AND JUST TRANSITIONS

In Chapter 4, we indicated that Simon Mcgrath et al.'s (2020) "emergent approach/model" to skills for African development offers much for shaping thinking about possible ways forward in imagining the relationships between the informal economy and workers, skills and training and the possibilities of moving towards decent work and just transitions. The development and framing of their model is "part of a larger project to develop new theories and practices of transformed VET from transformative development in African contexts". This larger project is framed by two intents in this particular article. In the first instance, it emerges from an engagement with, and review of, "existing literatures as a way of building towards new accounts of VET for African development" (McGrath et al., 2020, p. 466). In doing this work they "review the past by examining the major strands of the existing VET literature in/on Africa and critiquing these". This critique suggests that the "majority literatures of African VET are grounded in an inadequate theorisation of both VET and development". This limited theoretical development is unable, they suggest, to "fully account for political economy histories emerging out of colonial regimes that shape both what is present and what is absent in VET policies and debates". This absence of a focus on the political economy of African VET and development fails to provide insights that could drive research on VET, skills development and LLL "forward in the directions and at the pace necessary to confront the accelerating challenges faced". While this is important work, our interest here is with the second of their two aims, in which they seek to "imagine the future by offering a reflexive attempt to contribute to a transformed and transformative way of thinking about VET and sustainable development" (McGrath et al., 2020, p. 466).

In this context, their imagining of the future emerges from an investment in identifying and examining "new ways of approaching VET research that has potential to support the improvement of just livelihoods in Africa". These forms of research, practice and policy innovation, which we outline below, "point to ways in which VET can be theorised in relationship with economic, human and sustainable development, thus extending and expanding VET research in Africa" (McGrath et al., 2020, p. 472). Our sketch of these possible futures is provided with the sense that while these emerge from the particularities of diverse African contexts, they provide productive provocations for how to theorise VET and LLL's relationship with decent work, just transitions and sustainable development.

Policy, Systems and Institutions

McGrath et al. (2020, pp. 472–473) identify a theme in the research literature that is focused on "exploring the historical determinants influencing the shape of systems". This research, which appears as most productive in post-apartheid South Africa, "has begun exploring the colonial, settler and imperial foundations processes of policy borrowing, lending and transferring...and the nature of the economy underpinning the society". They suggest that this avenue of inquiry is "vital in emphasising the ways that systems evolve historically and reflect the complexities of national political-economic configurations". This emerging work "stresses the need to investigate system dynamics for the obstacles and opportunities that will shape the likely success of innovations designed to make VET more inclusive and sustainable". Examples here include, Volker Wedekind's (2014, 2018) work examining the challenges and opportunities for institutionalised TVET systems in post-apartheid South Africa, and for institutionalised skills training, given South Africa's relatively small, and "stagnant" formal labour market.

In the previous chapter we reported on work we had undertaken in reviewing the emergence, impact and limits and possibilities of TVET policies, systems and institutions in shaping the promise of LLL for decent work and just transitions in the Asia–Pacific region—with a particular focus on the impacts of the COVID-19 pandemic on this promise (Phillips, 2020). That work reflects, in a number of significant ways, the need to identify and analyse the "system dynamics" in particular contexts, in order to examine "the obstacles and opportunities that will shape the likely success of innovations designed to make VET more inclusive and sustainable". For example, in Small Island Developing Countries (SIDCs) in the Pacific, a significant priority by UNESCO (2018, p. 57) was that "TVET sectors, through the appropriate national governance and management structures, are supported through the provision of policy advice, technical assistance and skills reinforcement to review and reposition the sector to provide relevant, quality seamless learning pathways and lifelong learning opportunities". These UNESCO priorities for TVET were reflected in the national development priorities statements of the Pacific Island countries, as detailed in the "Part V Country focus and alignment of development" section of the UNESCO *Pacific Strategy* (UNESCO, 2018, pp. 67–143). Similar TVET priorities were also evident in the *Pacific Regional Education Framework (PacREF) 2018–2030: Moving Towards Education 2030*, which covers 17 Pacific island countries as well as Australia and New Zealand. The PacREF, in part, recognises the importance of partnerships in the region with agencies like "the Australia Pacific Technical College (APTC), that have made and are making significant contributions to Pacific education and training outcomes" (Pacific Islands Forum Secretariat, 2018, pp. 9–14).

And yet, even these sorts of investments and partnerships do not necessarily guarantee that TVET and LLL will fulfil the skills development aspirations of young people and informal workers in SIDCs. During the pandemic, in the Pacific region, "informal workers, as well as those with low work-from-home or high physical proximity service jobs" were negatively impacted (Arahan et al., 2020, p. 13). Similarly, jobs that were customer-facing were "particularly prone to disruption", as were jobs "often occupied by workers with lower levels of education". As women and young people were predominantly employed in informal work, the impact of the pandemic on them disproportionately "exacerbated existing inequalities in the world of work" (Arahan et al., 2020, p. 13).

Vocational Knowledge

Another theme in the literature points to the need to get beyond "crude technical approaches to what skills appear to be needed at the surface level, and to consider what knowledge, as well as skills, is required for transformative VET". This research highlights the affinities to both the "community development approach's Freirean roots, and to the sustainable development approach's emphasis on participatory, inclusive knowledge formation and on boundary-crossing learning". Here, they reference recent research by Jeanne Gamble (2018), who suggests that competency-based approaches to TVET in South Africa have "derived from rudimentary labour market analyses". Gamble's research suggests, in contrast, "that labour process analysis reveals how different jobs with the same title are often very different and how the nature of knowledge used at work differs dramatically within the same ostensible occupational role" (McGrath et al., 2020, pp. 473–474).

In recent work (Goring & Kelly, in press) we have developed an extensive review and analysis of the ways in which powerful, abstract discourses of young people's twenty-first-century skills are mobilised, in diverse ways, across the globe as means to identify the skills and capabilities that young people need to develop to secure more secure forms of employment in globalised, precarious worlds of work. We trace the World Economic Forum's *The Future of Jobs Report* series (WEF, 2016, 2018, 2020) that develops the concept of the Fourth Industrial Revolution (4IR) in which the futures of work are made knowable in terms of the automation of routine labour, globalisation, the increased flexibilisation of work, uncertain and changing labour markets and digital disruption. For Klaus Schwab (2017, p. 8), the WEF's founder, the Fourth Industrial Revolution is fundamentally different from previous revolutions due to the "fusion and interaction of technologies" from "gene sequencing to nanotechnology, from renewables to quantum computing" across "physical, digital and biological domains". In his work, Schwab (2017, p. 8) acknowledges the unequal distribution of these transformations to economic and social life, when he observes that the "second industrial revolution has yet to be fully experienced by 17% of the world as nearly 1.3 billion people still lack access to electricity". The WEF's imagining of the future of work, jobs, skills and education are significant to the production and reproduction of discourses of twenty-first-century skills, which it poses as a solution to these cycles of economic and technological change.

In that work we are interested in examining some of the limits and possibilities for the production of these versions of futures in what we call a "neoliberal education apparatus". In the first instance, we argue that these futures are produced as knowable, technical problems to be solved through the development of young people's twenty-first-century enterprise skills, and their aspirations towards futures of work imagined in these terms. Knowledges of the impacts and trajectories of neoliberal economic deregulation and deindustrialisation, and policies impacting young people's experiences of a crisis of precarious work in different places are, largely, made absent in these discourses through their focus on abstract sets of skills that are grouped in the following ways:

> *Foundational Literacies*—Literacy, Numeracy, Scientific Literacy, ICT Literacy, Financial Literacy, Civic and Cultural Literacy.
> *Competencies*—Critical Thinking/Problem Solving, Creativity, Communication, Collaboration.

Character Qualities—Curiosity, Initiative, Persistence/Grit, Adaptability, Leadership, Social and Cultural Awareness (WEF, 2016).

In a number of projects our aim, which mirrors Gamble's (2018) concerns, is to identify these, problematic, abstract and de-contextualised understandings of twenty-first-century skills as a space of departure to critically rethink, and explore the limits and opportunities afforded by this manner of categorising, compartmentalising, quantifying and disaggregating the diverse range of attributes and capabilities that are deemed essential for young people's "employability" in increasingly precarious and uncertain futures of work. In these projects we are seeking to contribute to a more critical and productive interjection into debates about skills, capabilities and young people's education training and employment pathways. And to think creatively about the "social life" of these skills, what these *Foundational Literacies, Competencies* and *Character Qualities* might mean in different social, cultural and work contexts, the forms of "value" that they signify, the ways in which this value might be translated, and the time scales over which these 'skills' hold these different forms of "value" (Kelly, 2023).

Critical Capabilities Approach (CCA) and VET for Community Development

McGrath et al. (2020, pp. 474–476) also identify an emergent interest in two distinct, but closely related, approaches to the relationships between VET and decent work and just transitions. In the first instance, what they identify as the *critical capabilities approach* (CCA) draws on fields such as a political economy of skills tradition, critical realism and feminist theory to move "beyond the atomised individualism of the orthodox human capital approach by developing a far stronger account of agency", and earlier "work on capabilities and education by insisting on the importance of structure and power". Research in this space seeks to focus on "both inequality in skills development and how we move away from a narrow focus on immediate employability and production". In relation to how VET is often positioned as a panacea to youth under- and unemployment, they argue that the CCA has a "strong focus both on the need to give considerable attention to young people's voices in articulating their aspirations for meaningful work and lives, and on their intersectional experience of marginalisation and disempowerment".

McGrath et al. (2020, pp. 474–476) identify how the CCA has eight key elements related to understanding people's relationships to skills development and VET:

1. Poverty—"it insists on foregrounding poverty in order to better understand many young people's challenging lived experiences".
2. Gender—the approach draws on feminist literatures to "stress how women experience intersectional disadvantages that shape the decisions that they make about education and work throughout their lives and the outcomes they achieve".
3. Political Economy—a focus on how "structural reality influences individuals' experiences of VET".
4. Work—"insists on a broad conception of work. It argues that work is not only about income/production but should also be about self-identity and self-worth".
5. Learner Aspirations—a primary interest for VET and VET research "should be on how it supports what individuals want to pursue in order to flourish". Here, evidence "from South Africa suggests that VET learners are not simply concerned with immediate employability but value other outcomes from their VET participation, such as respect, active citizenship and empowerment".
6. Aspirations—understands aspirations as "forward-looking 'life projects' in which individuals attempt to respond to their structural obstacles and their endowments of various resources in order to imagine and achieve better lives".
7. Life Projects and Decision Points—"the reassessment of life projects and adjustment of aspirations occurs as a repeated process. It draws attention to the series of decision points that individuals experience regarding their learning and work trajectories".
8. Success—evaluation should "focus primarily on the extent and ways in which institutions, and the system, support the flourishing of learners".

In a related theme, McGrath et al. (2020, pp. 476–477) suggest that a focus on *VET for Community Development* takes up many of the same concerns in the CCA, and further references key interests of a "critical adult education" tradition. They identify two main African hubs for this approach: "the Youth, Education and Work (YEW) network, centred on the UNESCO Chair in Lifelong Learning, Youth and Work at Gulu University in Uganda...and a radical adult and community education tradition in South Africa". In discussing the example of Uganda, and the work being done there, they suggest that historically there has been a "governmental and aid agency emphasis on access and enrolment in education" and not enough attention to the "systematic dynamics of inequality". In emphasising so-called "opportunity", this institutional and "orthodox approach to education and development has prioritised access and underplayed the structural factors that cause drop out". They reference a variety of work from the YEW network that indicates that an "over-academic education, high levels of drop out and massive levels of youth unemployment force young Ugandans into indecent work". In this approach, and the traditions that it draws on, there is a focus on such things as participatory action research; "valuing and acting upon local knowledges including those of rural people and the youth"; and an interest in "local socio-economic contexts, attitudes and aspirations" as these shape the possibilities of a transformative approach to VET.

As we demonstrated in our provocation in Chapter 6—where we drew on previous work on *COVID-19 and the (Broken) Promise of Education for Sustainable Development: A Case Study from Post-colonial Pakistan* (Anwar et al., 2023)—these challenges are also evident in other postcolonial development contexts such as Pakistan. In the Global Competitive Index, for example, the World Economic Forum has ranked Pakistan 125th in "education and skills", and 127th in "ICT adoption" pillars, out of 140 countries (Schwab, 2018, p. 448). As we have suggested in that book (Anwar et al., 2023, pp. 37–39) Pakistan's ranking in these indices points to a lack of access to decent work and productive employment (Pakistan Bureau of Statistics, 2012). Pakistan also lacks the capacity to produce a skilled workforce with 60% of its population (around 120 million people) below the age of 18 (Ministry of Federal Education and Training, MoFEPT, 2018). In the next thirty years, the working-age population of the country will double. Keeping in view these concerns and the commitments to global development frameworks and agenda, Pakistan has struggled to construct a curriculum, and/or to implement adequate educational systems and structures to provide young people with skills and knowledge needed for sustainable engagement with global economic processes and systems. UNESCO (2015) argues that technical and vocational education and training (TVET) is fundamental to sustainable economic and social development through the development of productive capacity of young people and adults. These sorts of claims suggest that enhancing young people's skills through quality education and training are vital in addressing skill shortages according to the changing market demands, as well as increasing youth unemployment in postcolonial development contexts such as Pakistan.

However, and in ways that mirror the observations of McGrath et al. (2020), significant aspects of Pakistan's education system are not aligned with the current market demands for so-called twenty-first-century skills, which reduces young people's chances of employability, and does not significantly contribute to the sustainable development objectives of poverty reduction, decent work and just transitions (Wedmann & Iqbal, 2017). Nearly two decades ago the Governor of the State Bank of Pakistan indicated a mismatch between the emerging needs of the economy and scarce supply of skilled and educated workforce in the country (Hussain, 2005). This lack of preparedness, compounded by the low quality of the education system, leads to high levels of "drop out" and alienation from schools (Khan, 2009). Pakistan participated in Trends in International Maths and Science Study (TIMSS) in 2019 but still does not participate in the Program for International Student Assessment (PISA) (Abdullah, 2020). Young people's aptitude, knowledge and skills, in themselves, and in comparison to other countries, are yet to be determined. The national education assessment system also measures rote learning rather than analytical skills and critical thinking. There is also evidence of cheating during exams, bribery and corruption, parents' influences and political interference in the processes of literacy skills assessment (Gouleta, 2015). Parents in Pakistan, as elsewhere, exert significant influence on young people's decisions about their career pathways, whether to continue undergraduate or university education, or to pursue a career in technical and vocational education and training (Ayub, 2017). Income, earning and high social status are other factors that influence the young people's career choices (Sharif et al., 2019). Students' interest, their aptitude and their willingness and/or unwillingness to opt for a TVET pathway, is little considered, and there are few counselling mechanisms for parents and students in this regard.

Skills for Sustainable Development

McGrath et al.'s (2020, pp. 477-479) final theme emerges from global, national and more local moves to theorise the relationship between VET, skills development and the emerging agenda for sustainable development. They situate this theme in a number of historical and emerging challenges related to Africa's colonial histories, and the postcolonial legacies that continue to name and respond to "the negative effects of the colonial and Apartheid land expropriation or extractivism". Recent attempts to take up the opportunities and challenges of a global agenda for sustainable development encounter the legacies of the "bifurcation of skills formation systems between an industrial-focused VET mainstream and a separate agricultural and natural resource management focused skills system that reflected the unequal access to and ownership of land". They indicate that in a number of projects "more complex theoretical perspectives on the phenomenon of green skills and VET in Africa are emerging". These perspectives reference traditions and approaches such as "critical realism, political ecology theory, sociology and development studies, as well as on transformative learning and curriculum theory and praxis". In addition, this approach has a focus on the "political economies of knowledge production", that seeks to foreground "exclusions" such as "the absence of sustainable agricultural curricula from much of conventional, industrial VET".

One example here references the work of Heila Lotz-Sisitka and her colleagues (Lotz-Sisitka et al., 2016, p. iii) in South Africa whose work is "oriented towards a systemic, innovation oriented and relational approach to knowledge dissemination". Their purpose was to "further the objectives of knowledge co-construction and social innovation in the area of rainwater harvesting and conservation (RWH&C) for food production at household and smallholder farmer level". This project was based in a "Strategy-as-Practice" framework that foregrounded "the interrelations between people and practice in the emergence of strategy". As McGrath et al. (2020, p. 478) suggest, this sort of work points to the need to locate TVET "in a more regionally contextualised frame, where theoretical knowledge is grounded and reflexively constituted in relation to practices". Such an approach recognises a need to focus on the "formation of new knowledge in education, and the creation of new human activities that reflect the intersections of society-nature-economy, tradition and innovation, and that are more inclusive". Importantly, in terms of the ways in which many of these approaches are grounded in local, place-based, critical, emancipatory and (socio-)ecological understandings of livelihood, work, skills and training:

> these accounts point to the need to look more into how individuals and communities form aspirations about how productive work supports better lives and what place vocational learning can play in this. However, they also point towards the necessity of understanding how attitudes of learners, parents and employers are shaped both by economic signals and by their perceptions about the value of different forms of learning, knowledge and qualifications. Some of these accounts raise important questions about how both VET's current status and potential to play a transformative role are dependent on issues of knowledge and learning and how these are structured by the effects of power. (McGrath et al., 2020, p. 481)

Arjun Appadurai's (2004) influential essay, *The Capacity to Aspire: Culture and the Terms of Recognition*, provides a useful addendum to McGrath et al.'s observations here. Appadurai (2004) argues that in order to understand the continuation of extreme poverty, disadvantage and marginalisation, and why people who live in these conditions appear—to some commentators, politicians and communities—not to "aspire" for a "better life", then we need to shift focus from the individual and their "failings". As he suggests:

> I am not saying that the poor cannot wish, want, need, plan, or aspire. But part of poverty is a diminishing of the circumstances in which these practices occur. If the map of aspirations…is seen to consist of a dense combination of nodes and pathways, relative poverty means a smaller number of aspirational nodes and a thinner, weaker sense of the pathways from concrete wants to intermediate contexts to general norms and back again. (Appadurai, 2004, p. 69)

In a number of spaces, in our empirical and theoretical work on young people, their education, training and employment pathways, their health and well-being, their sense of their futures and their anxieties and uncertainties, their hopes and aspirations in relation to these futures, we have used Appadurai's concerns to problematise the ways in which various agencies—such as the OECD (Mann et al., 2020) in their *Dream Jobs?* report—imagine the problem of young people and the futures of work (see, for example Goring et al., 2023; Kelly, 2022).

In those spaces, we have suggested that to be "aspirational" can be understood as a "moral disposition" that young people should develop towards the possible relationships between their pasts, presents and futures. In this sense, young people's ability to be "aspirational" is largely understood in terms of education, training and employment pathways—which are imagined as being more or less "linear", and with some "end point" in mind, where they have become "aligned" with the "jobs of the future" (Mann et al., 2020). This is a moral disposition that is accompanied by an obligation to imagine these futures in large part through the frameworks and ideas of significant "others"—families, adults, teachers, schools, governments, businesses and communities. In *The Capacity to Aspire* Appadurai (2004, pp. 68–69) argues that we need to think about the ways in which a person or community's social, cultural and economic circumstances can produce particular "orientations to the future":

> But here is the twist with the capacity to aspire. It is not evenly distributed in any society. It is a sort of meta capacity, and the relatively rich and powerful invariably have a more fully developed capacity to aspire. What does this mean? It means that the better off you are (in terms of power, dignity, and material resources), the more likely you are to be conscious of the links between the more and less immediate objects of aspiration.

Drawing on Appadurai's ideas about the capacity to aspire, and in listening to the voices of young people in a number of projects, we have been encouraged to shift our focus from the "aspirations" of individual young people who might be marginalised, disengaged or from an area of historical disadvantage—and how we might "fix" their misaligned sense of the "future of work". And to think, instead, about the different resources (economic, social and cultural capital), family contexts and relations, ideas, role models, peers and peer networks, opportunities, intelligences and abilities, bodily abilities and disabilities and histories that might be at play in shaping the complex and uncertain relationships and contexts in which young people live, imagine who they are and what they might be and become.

The challenge and opportunity here is to *imagine* how far some of these proposals, approaches and models might "travel"—both within Africa, and to the other regions and countries that we have been focused on here. Given the urgency of the convergence of the aftermath of the pandemic, the unfolding and unequal consequences of the climate crisis, the increasing scale, scope and experience of informal work in informal economies on the margins of globalising capitalism—that is amplified by the "decent" work replacing technological revolutions heralded by the emergence and spread of forms of artificial and machine intelligence— the rolling crisis of hundreds of millions of internally displaced people, and refugee and migrant populations, and the rise of extremist, totalitarian social, cultural and political responses to this world of "permacrisis" (European Policy Centre, 2021) and "polycrisis" (Torkington, 2023), there is a profound need to engage in a radical re-imagining of how to deliver on the promise of LLL for decent work and just transitions. Our work here on a political economy of LLL for decent work and just transitions has made a modest contribution to that ongoing radical re-imagining.

REFERENCES

Abdullah, N. A. (2020). The state of education in Pakistan: An analytical overview of basic education indicators. *New Horizons, 14*(1), 1–14. https://www.proquest.com/scholarly-journals/state-education-pakistan-analytical-review-basic/docview/2435482930/se-2

Allam, M., Ader, M., & Igrioglu, G. (2020). *Youth and COVID-19: Response, recovery and resilience.* https://www.oecd.org/coronavirus/policy-responses/youth-and-covid-19-response-recovery-and-resilience-c40e61c6/

Anwar, J., Khan, S. R., Shah, M. Z., Brown, S., Kelly, P., & Phillips, S. (2023). *COVID-19 and the (broken) promise of education for sustainable development: A case study from postcolonial Pakistan* (Vol. 7). Brill. https://brill.com/display/title/64453

Appadurai, A. (2004). The capacity to aspire: Culture and the terms of recognition. In D. Held & H. L. Moore (Eds.), *Cultural politics in a global age: Uncertainty, solidarity and innovation* (pp. 59–84). Oneworld Publication.

Arahan, R., Doan, D., Dornan, M., Munoz, A., Parsons, K., & Yi, S. (2020). *Pacific Island countries in the era of COVID-19: Macroeconomic impacts and job prospects* (The World Bank Group, Issue). https://www.voced.edu.au/content/ngv%3A92829

Ayub, H. (2017). Parental influence and attitude of students towards technical education and vocational training. *International Journal of Information and Education Technology, 7*(7), 534–538. https://www.ijiet.org/vol7/925-ME1001.pdf

European Policy Centre. (2021). *Europe in the age of permacrisis.* European Policy Centre. https://www.epc.eu/en/Publications/Europe-in-the-age-of-permacrisis~3c8a0c

Freire, P. (1972). *Pedagogy of the oppressed*. Penguin.
Gamble, J. (2018). From labour market to labour process: Finding a basis for curriculum in TVET. *International Journal of Training Research, 14*(3), 215–229. https://doi.org/10.1080/14480220.2016.1254367
Goring, J., & Kelly, P. (in press). *On the problem of young people and uncertain futures*. Routledge.
Goring, J., Kelly, P., Padilla, D. C., & Brown, S. (2023). Young people's presents and futures, and the moral obligation to be enterprising and aspirational in times of crisis. *Futures, 147*, 103099. https://doi.org/10.1016/j.futures.2023.103099
Gouleta, E. (2015). Educational assessment in Khyber Pakhtunkhwa Pakistan's North-West frontier province: Practices, issues, and challenges for educating culturally linguistically diverse and exceptional children. *Global Education Review, 2*(4), 19–39.
Guterres, A. (2021). *Secretary-General calls latest IPCC Climate Report 'Code Red for Humanity'*. Retrieved 29 August from https://press.un.org/en/2021/sgsm20847.doc.htm
Hussain, I. (2005). Education, employment and economic development in Pakistan. In R. M. Hathaway (Ed.), *Education reform in Pakistan: Building for the future* (pp. 33–45). Woodrow Wilson International Center for Scholars. https://www.wilsoncenter.org/sites/default/files/media/documents/publication/FinalPDF.pdf
Kelly, P. (2022). *Aspiration and young people's sense of their futures in the time of COVID*. Young People's Sustainable Futures Lab. Retrieved 1 July from https://youngpeoplesfutureslab.org/aspiration-and-young-peoples-sense-of-their-futures-in-the-time-of-covid/https://youngpeoplesfutureslab.org/aspiration-and-young-peoples-sense-of-their-futures-in-the-time-of-covid/
Kelly, P. (2023). *Young people, 21st Century Skills and the future of work*. Vital Arts: Skilling Young People for the Future. Retrieved 1 July from https://vital-arts.org/blog/21st-century-skills
Khan, S. H. (2009). Making people employable: Reforming secondary education in Pakistan. *The Pakistan Development Review, 48*(4), 603–617. https://www.jstor.org/stable/41261337
Lotz-Sisitka, H., Pesanayi, T., Weaver, K., Lupele, C., Sisitka, L., O'Donoghue, R., Sithole, P., van Staden, W., Denison, C. M. J., & Phillips, K. (2016). *Water use and food security: Knowledge dissemination and use in agricultural colleges and local learning networks for homestead food gardening and smallholder farming*. Research and Development Report: Report to the Water Research Commission. Water Research Commission. https://vital.seals.ac.za/vital/access/manager/Repository/vital:73308?site_name=GlobalView&view=list&f0=sm_creator%3A%22van+Staden%2C+Wilna%22&sort=ss_dateNormalized+asc%2Csort_ss_title+asc

Mann, A., Denis, V., Schleicher, A., Ekhtiari, H., Forsyth, T., Liu, E., & Chambers, N. (2020). *Dream jobs? Teenagers' career aspirations and the future of work*. https://www.inspiring-girls.it/wp-content/uploads/2020/01/Davos2020Embargo22Jan.pdf

Mayo, P. (1994). Synthesizing Gramsci and Freire: Possibilities for a theory of radical adult education. *International Journal of Lifelong Education, 13*(2), 125–148. https://doi.org/10.1080/0260137940130204

McGrath, S., Ramsarup, P., Zeelen, J., Wedekind, V., Allais, S., Lotz-Sisitka, H., Monk, D., Openjuru, G., & Russon, J.-A. (2020). Vocational education and training for African development: A literature review. *Journal of Vocational Education & Training, 72*(4), 465–487. https://doi.org/10.1080/13636820.2019.1679969

Ministry of Federal Education & Professional Training, MoFEPT. (2018). *National "skills for all" strategy: A roadmap for skill development in Pakistan*. Government of Pakistan. https://navttc.gov.pk/wp-content/uploads/2022/06/National-Skills-for-All-Strategy-2018.pdf

Pacific Islands Forum Secretariat. (2018). *Pacific regional education framework (PacREF) 2018-2030: Moving towards education 2030*. https://forumsec.org/publications/pacific-regional-education-framework-pacref-2018-2030-moving-towards-education-2030

Pakistan Bureau of Statistics. (2012). *Pakistan employment trends 2011. Progress towards achieving MDG target 1B "full and productive employment and decent work for all"*. https://www.pbs.gov.pk/sites/default/files/labour_force/publications/Pakistan_Employment_2012.pdf

Phillips, S. K. (2020). *Strengthening technical and vocational education and training (TVET) in Pacific small island developing countries (SIDCs) post COVID-19*. Retrieved 17 June from https://unevocrmit.wordpress.com/2020/12/02/strengthening-technical-and-vocational-education-and-training-tvet-in-pacific-small-island-developing-countries-sidcs-post-covid-19/

Schwab, K. (2017). *The Fourth Industrial Revolution*. Crown Currency.

Schwab, K. (2018). *The global competitiveness report 2018* (9295044762). https://www3.weforum.org/docs/GCR2018/05FullReport/

Sharif, N., Ahmad, N., & Sarwar, S. (2019). Factors influencing career choices. *IBT Journal of Business Studies, 15*(1), 33–46. https://ssrn.com/abstract=3431911

The Lancet. (2022). *Future child programme*. Retrieved 29 August from https://www.thelancet.com/campaigns/child-adolescent-health

Thompson, E. P. (1968). *The making of the English working class*. Pelican Books.

Torkington, S. (2023, January 13). *We're on the brink of a 'polycrisis'—How worried should we be?* World Economic Forum. Retrieved 1 July from https://www.weforum.org/agenda/2023/01/polycrisis-global-risks-report-cost-of-living/

Torres, C. A., & Yan, L. (2022). Paulo Freire and the state-of-the-art of the international journal of lifelong education. Invited article in celebration of 40 years of IJLE. *International Journal of Lifelong Education, 41*(6), 651–665. https://doi.org/10.1080/02601370.2022.2164435

UNESCO. (2015). *Incheon declaration: Education 2030: Towards inclusive and equitable quality education and lifelong learning for all.* http://uis.unesco.org/en/files/education-2030-incheon-framework-action-implementation-sdg4-2016-en-pdf-1

UNESCO. (2018). *Pacific strategy 2018–2022.* https://unesdoc.unesco.org/ark:/48223/pf0000366463

UNDESA. (2019). *SDG progress reports 2019: Are we on track to achieve the global goals?* https://www.un.org/development/desa/en/news/sustainable/sdg-progress-reports-2019.html

Wedekind, V. (2014). Going around in circles: Employability, responsiveness, and the reform of the college sector. In E. Motala (Ed.), *Education, economy & society* (pp. 57–80). University of South Africa Press. https://doi.org/10.25159/855-9

Wedekind, V. (2018). The idealisation of apprenticeship. In S. Allais & Y. Shalem (Eds.), *Knowledge, curriculum, and preparation for work* (pp. 104–126). Brill.

Wedmann, W. F., & Iqbal, A. (2017). *Study on producing skilled workforce for potential economic sectors in Balochistan.* https://tvetreform.org.pk/wp-content/uploads/downloads/pse/Summary%20Sector%20Studies.pdf

World Economic Forum. (2016). *The future of jobs: Employment, skills and workforce strategy for the Fourth Industrial Revolution.* https://www3.weforum.org/docs/WEF_Future_of_Jobs.pdf

World Economic Forum. (2018). *The future of jobs report.* https://www3.weforum.org/docs/WEF_Future_of_Jobs_2018.pdf

World Economic Forum. (2020). *The future of jobs report.* https://www3.weforum.org/docs/WEF_Future_of_Jobs_2020.pdf

Index

A
African
  development bank, 52, 74
  union, 74–76
Agency, 11, 12, 55
Allais, S., 15, 78, 152
Alla-Mensah, J., 8, 72
Altinyelken, H.K., 131
Amnesty International, 67
Anne-Marie, O.N, 131
Anwar, J., 127, 149
Appadurai, A., 152, 153
Apprentices, 56, 118
Arab Spring, 44, 62
Arab states, 5, 7, 47, 49
Arab Studies Institute (ASI), 10, 11
Asia-Pacific (AP), 4, 6, 13, 16, 117, 118, 122, 126, 140

B
Ball, S.J., 131
Basto-Aguirre, N., 13, 26–28
Bauman, Z., 2, 3, 9, 11, 57, 91
  wasted lives, 91

Beck, U., 6, 11
  Brazilianisation, 6
  The risk society, 6
Benvenuti, B., 109
Biles, J.J., 35, 36, 40
Braidotti, R., 5
Brown, S., 127, 149, 152

C
Capitalocene, 77, 85, 140
Central and Eastern Europe (CEE), 4, 6, 13, 96, 106, 140
Chang, D., 52–54, 59
Chen, M., 61, 118
Codd, J., 131
Co-design, 61, 105
Community-based, 102, 114
  approaches, 103
Conscientisation, 109
Council for Foreign Relations, 35
COVID-19 pandemic, 4, 5, 26, 28, 31, 58, 67, 91, 96, 98, 103, 124, 127, 138, 144

Critical capabilities approach (CCA), 17, 147

D
Decent work, 9, 12, 25, 31, 36, 55, 60, 62, 63, 65, 69, 71, 80, 90, 97, 108, 109, 126, 139–144, 149, 154
Department of Foreign Affairs and Trade (DFAT), 120
Deregulation, 36, 39, 146
Deutsche Gesellschaft für Internationale Zusammenarbeit (GIZ), 55, 121
Digital
  innovations, 122
  revolutions, 59
  skills, 104

E
Education
  formal, 29, 99, 118, 130
  non-formal, 29, 76
  The promise of, 117
  youth in transition from, 101
Employment, 6–8, 13–16, 26, 30–32, 48–50, 53, 60, 69, 73, 91, 96, 97, 99, 104, 107, 108, 117, 119, 127–129, 140, 153
  unemployment, 3, 36, 54, 71, 98, 99, 106, 128, 150
European
  commission, 68, 69
  network on debt and development (Eurodad), 23, 35
  policy centre, 138, 154
  union, 55, 90
European Centre for the Development of Vocational Training (Cedefop), 99

F
Formal
  certification, 73, 129
  economy, 104, 139
  sector, 5, 7, 15, 50, 54, 73, 79, 96, 98, 99, 107, 117, 140
  training, 105
  workers, 101, 102, 139
  workforce, 61
Fourth Industrial Revolution, 12, 14, 48, 57
Freire, P.
  co-create knowledge, 108
  conscientisation, 109
  critical
    interventions, 109
    reflection, 108
  liberating education, 108
  lived experiences, 108
  pedagogy of the oppressed, 108
  practices of dialogue, 108
Furlong, A., 6

G
Global capitalism, 57, 77, 110
Glovackas, S., 98
Goring, J., 146, 152
Guven, M., 14, 71

H
Harrison, L., 2
Harvey, J., 61

I
Informal
  activities, 72
  apprenticeships, 54, 56, 72, 73, 104, 118, 119
  economy, 5–8, 13–16, 26, 27, 29, 30, 35, 36, 47, 48, 50, 58, 61, 69, 71–74, 77, 78, 96, 97,

101, 103–105, 115, 117–121, 123, 126, 138, 139, 143
employment, 7, 8, 14–16, 27, 28, 32, 33, 48–51, 70, 71, 90, 96, 98, 101, 106–108, 114, 118, 122, 141
firms, 99, 122
labour, 14, 16, 26, 36, 39, 47, 48, 69, 77, 97, 98, 106, 138, 140, 141
on-the-job-training, 30, 56, 73, 119
organisations, 8, 13, 16, 26, 37, 96, 97, 104, 105, 119, 139
sector, 5, 7, 13, 15, 26, 28, 29, 54, 61, 72–74, 97, 98, 102, 103, 114, 115, 117–119, 121, 140
skills, 118
training, 13, 14, 17, 31, 52, 54, 55, 57, 59, 71, 73, 74, 97, 99–104, 108, 117–119, 121, 143
work, 7, 35, 36, 40, 69, 71, 72, 91, 98, 102, 106, 107, 126, 139–141, 145, 154
workers, 4, 5, 7, 8, 12–14, 16, 26, 28, 30, 36, 39, 40, 46–49, 51, 52, 54–57, 59, 61, 63, 73, 77, 90, 96, 97, 99–104, 107–109, 114, 119, 122, 123, 126, 139–141, 145
Informality, 4–8, 14, 15, 27–29, 32, 49, 50, 70, 90, 97, 101
International and development agencies, 51
International Labour Organization (ILO), 5, 7, 8, 14, 16, 25, 31, 37, 49–51, 53, 61, 71, 90, 96, 98, 101, 104, 117–119
International Monetary Fund (IMF), 4, 23, 25, 36, 54

K
Kanbur, R., 8, 14, 72
Kapoor, I., 77
Karlen, R., 14, 71
Kelly, P., 2, 6, 10, 11, 127, 131, 146, 147, 149, 152
Khan, S.R., 127, 149
Kiaga, A.K., 14, 15, 70, 71
Klein, N., 13, 26, 37–39
 disaster capitalism, 37

L
Lancet, 109, 138
Latin America and the Caribbean (LAC), 4, 6, 12, 13, 22, 25, 31, 139
Leung, V., 14, 15, 70, 71
Liberalization, 36
Lifelong Learning (LLL)
 capability, 118
 a political economy of, 9, 12, 13, 17, 26, 37, 40, 62, 80, 84, 109, 126, 131, 139–142, 154
 opportunities, 10, 16, 17, 48, 51, 59, 74, 84, 108, 126, 139, 141
 the broken promise of, 40, 127
Lotz-Sisitka, H., 15, 78, 152

M
Marshall-Denton, C., 109
Maurizio, R., 25, 26, 31–34
McCann, S., 109
McGrath, S., 8, 12, 15, 17, 72, 77–85, 143–145, 147, 148, 150–152
Middle East and North Africa (MENA), 4, 6, 12, 14, 46–48, 50–55, 57–59, 61, 62, 139
Migrants, 35, 51, 68, 91, 99, 109, 114, 116, 117, 131
Monk, D., 15, 78, 152

N

Nieto-Parra, S., 13, 26–28
Non-formal learning, 84, 99
Non-government organizations (NGOs), 23, 55, 56, 72, 73, 78, 82, 103, 127
Novelli, M., 131

O

Ohnsorge, F., 14, 48, 50, 54, 55
Olssen, M., 131
Openjuru, G., 15, 78, 152
Organization for Economic Co-operation and Development (OECD), 3, 4, 6, 13, 14, 27, 28, 51, 98, 99, 101–104, 119, 152

P

Pacific small island developing countries (SIDCs), 120, 123–125, 144, 145
Packard, T., 27, 39
Padilla, D.C., 152
Palmer, R., 9, 29, 30, 56, 59, 72, 73, 117–119, 123
Pfau-Effinger, B., 106, 107, 141
Phillips, S., 127, 149
Phillips, S.K., 123–125
Political economy, 9, 10, 12–14, 35, 37, 48, 57, 60, 61, 71, 84, 117, 139, 140, 143, 154
Postcolonial/post-Colonial
  development challenges, 77
  legacies, 71, 77, 130, 151
  Pakistan, 127, 130, 149, 150
  theories of development, 77
Privatization, 36, 39

R

Ramsarup, P., 15, 78, 152

Redundancy, 2–4, 140
Refugees, 15, 35, 49, 51, 91, 97
Robertson, R, 27, 39
Russon, J.-A., 15, 78, 152

S

Schwab, K., 146, 149
Shah, M.Z., 127, 149
Shehadeh, S., 52–54, 59
Silva, J., 27, 39
Skills
  development, 2, 26, 33, 40, 47, 52, 54–57, 59, 60, 69, 77, 83, 99, 100, 102, 104, 105, 108, 120, 124, 130, 139, 147, 151
  development systems, 52
  for sustainable development, 17, 151
  green, 51, 75, 83, 151
  training, 2, 4, 13, 17, 29–31, 71, 74, 82, 83, 102, 103, 118, 119, 144
Social
  protection, 16, 34, 36, 49, 61, 97, 104, 106–108, 115, 117, 140
  welfare systems, 108
Solidarity Center, 23, 24
Sousa, L., 27, 39
Sub-Saharan Africa (SSA), 4, 6, 13–15, 69–71, 72, 74, 75, 77, 78, 81, 139
Sustainable
  Africa, 74
  development, 5, 6, 8, 9, 12, 69, 71, 74, 78, 79, 121, 127, 138, 144, 150
Swilling, M., 12, 40, 63, 80

T

Technical and Vocational Education and Training (TVET)

programs, 54, 124
qualifications, 125
systems, 52, 53, 59, 144
Thompson, E.P., 44, 62, 141
history from below, 44, 62, 141

U
United Nations
Children's Fund (UNICEF), 119
Conference on Trade and
Development, 67
Department of Economic and Social
Affairs (UNDESA), 40, 138
Development Program (UNDP),
74, 75
Economic and Social Commission
for Western Asia (ESCW), 48,
61
Educational, Scientific and Cultural
Organisation (UNESCO), 37,
52, 54, 105, 116, 118,
123–125, 144, 149
Millennium Development Goals
(MDGs), 78
Security Council (UNSC), 24
Sustainable Development Goals
(SDGs), 5, 12, 69, 74, 78
Women, 114, 115

V
Vázquez-Zamora, J., 13, 26–28
Verger, A., 131
Vocational Education and Training
(VET)
for community development, 17,
147, 148
knowledge, 145

W
Wedekind, V., 15, 78, 152
World Bank, 4, 13, 22, 26, 37, 39,
50, 55, 70, 76, 118, 121
World Economic Forum (WEF), 12,
71, 138, 146, 147, 149

Y
Young people, 2, 14, 29, 48, 55, 56,
59, 73, 76, 118, 119, 125–130,
145–147, 149, 150, 152, 153
Yu, S., 14, 48, 50, 54, 55

Z
Zeelen, J., 15, 78, 152

GPSR Compliance

The European Union's (EU) General Product Safety Regulation (GPSR) is a set of rules that requires consumer products to be safe and our obligations to ensure this.

If you have any concerns about our products, you can contact us on

ProductSafety@springernature.com

In case Publisher is established outside the EU, the EU authorized representative is:

Springer Nature Customer Service Center GmbH
Europaplatz 3
69115 Heidelberg, Germany

www.ingramcontent.com/pod-product-compliance
Lightning Source LLC
Chambersburg PA
CBHW061044231025
34251CB00056B/320